easy roasting

easy roasting

simply delicious recipes for your perfect roast

LONDON • NEW YORK

Designer Paul Stradling

Editors Ellen Parnavelas and Miriam Catley

Production Manager Gary Hayes

Art Director Leslie Harrington

Editorial Director Julia Charles

Indexer Hilary Bird

First published in 2012 by
Ryland Peters & Small
20–21 Jockey's Fields
London WC1R 4BW
and
Ryland Peters & Small, Inc.
519 Broadway, 5th Floor
New York, NY10012

www.rylandpeters.com

ISBN UK: 978 1 84975 255 8
10 9 8 7 6 5 4 3 2 1

ISBN US: 978 1 84975 284 8
10 9 8 7 6 5 4 3 2 1

Text © Valerie Aikman-Smith, Ghillie Basan, Fiona
Beckett, Maxine Clark, Ross Dobson, Clare Ferguson,
Brian Glover, Alastair Hendy, Sonia Stevenson, Fran
Warde, Laura Washburn, Lindy Wildsmith and Ryland
Peters & Small 2012

Design and photographs © Ryland Peters & Small 2012

The recipes in this book have been published previously
by Ryland Peters & Small.

A CIP record for this book is available from the
British Library.

US Library of Congress cataloging-in-publication data
has been applied for.

Printed in China

Notes

• All spoon measurements are level unless otherwise
specified.

• Weights and measurements have been rounded up
or down slightly to make measuring easier.

• Eggs are UK medium/US large unless otherwise
specified. Uncooked or partly cooked eggs should
not be served to the very young, the very old, those
with compromised immune systems or to pregnant
women.

• Ovens should be preheated to the specified
temperature. Recipes in this book were tested using
a regular oven. If using a fan-assisted oven, follow
the manufacturer's instructions for adjusting
temperatures.

• When a recipe calls for the grated zest of citrus
fruit, buy unwaxed fruit and wash well before using.
If you can only find treated fruit, scrub well in warm
soapy water and rinse before using.

contents

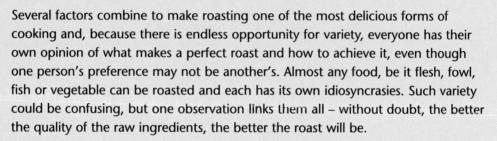

warm, convivial, family food ...

A roast is always special. It makes a warm, convivial meal that's perfect for family get togethers on weekends – or for special occasions like Christmas, Thanksgiving, birthdays or anniversaries. It's the sort of meal that memories are made of – most people remember fondly the roasts their mothers cooked for Sunday lunch.

Several factors combine to make roasting one of the most delicious forms of cooking and, because there is endless opportunity for variety, everyone has their own opinion of what makes a perfect roast and how to achieve it, even though one person's preference may not be another's. Almost any food, be it flesh, fowl, fish or vegetable can be roasted and each has its own idiosyncrasies. Such variety could be confusing, but one observation links them all – without doubt, the better the quality of the raw ingredients, the better the roast will be.

Roasting is a very Western form of cooking. The domestic oven was developed in the nineteenth century. Before that, except for the huge spits found in big houses, most family cooking was done in a pot over an open fire. The early domestic oven, with its ability to control temperature, albeit in a very primitive way, meant that the roast gradually became the quintessential family meal. Modern ovens, often convection to keep the air and heat circulating more evenly around the food, have all the safeguards that our ancestors lacked. You will need an even source of heat that can be readily altered to accommodate the different styles of roasting in this book.

A method as basic as roasting is really simplicity itself and with quality ingredients, a good source of steady heat, and the recipes in this book, how can you fail?

7

roasting know-how

It is useful to follow a routine when you prepare meat and poultry for roasting:

• Weigh the roast if necessary and calculate the cooking time, using either the tables for roasting (page 19, 21) or by following the times given in the recipe. If you're buying from a supermarket or similar source, the weight will be given on the packaging. If the meat or poultry contains a stuffing, that must be included in the total weight.

• Remove the roast from the refrigerator and let it return to room temperature at least 30 minutes before cooking.

• At the same time, set the oven to the starting heat (some ovens can take up to 20 minutes to preheat). Check the temperature with an oven thermometer (many ovens are inaccurate).

• If the butcher has not already done so, the meat or bird should be trimmed and tied if necessary. Extra fat, such as pork fat, can be wrapped around very lean roasts, such as pheasants or lean beef, and tied with kitchen string to keep it in place.

• If cooking pork with crackling, score the skin into strips with a sharp knife. Alternatively, ask the butcher to do this for you when you buy it.

• Baste the meat with the chosen oil, butter or other fat to prevent the flesh or skin from drying out.

• Season with salt, pepper or seasoned flour as appropriate. This is optional – some people prefer not to season until later (or even at all).

• Put the roast directly in a roasting pan or, if there is going to be a lot of fat produced (as with duck or goose), set it on a rack in the pan so it doesn't fry in its own dripping. This will also let air circulate around the roast.

There is an ongoing debate as to whether roasting at high temperatures for a comparatively short time gives a better result than roasting at a lower temperature for a longer time with a couple of short high-temperature episodes at the start or finish of the cooking. There are cooks who swear by one method or the other, but in my opinion both methods have their pros and cons.

Fast-roasting
Only very tender cuts of meat are cooked at high temperatures. High heat shrinks meat fibres and toughens them, so anything that requires heat to tenderize it must opt for slow-roasting. At high temperatures, accurate timing is essential to reach the required internal temperature, whereas when cooking at a low temperature 10 minutes either way makes little difference.

If we look closely at the effect of a really hot oven – 230°C (450°F) Gas 8 – on a roast, it will show the internal juices being drawn to the surface where they evaporate, leaving a delicious concentrated coating on the outer surface. Inside, there is an edging of hot, well-cooked meat surrounding a mass of raw flesh in the centre and at this point, if the meat is 'rested' in a warm environment, such as a gentle plate-warming area, given time, the juices will redistribute themselves and the meat will be an even, rosy colour right through. This is an ideal way to cook meat to be served rare.

If left longer in the hot oven instead of being rested, the meat becomes progressively more cooked, drier and tougher, while the outside becomes seared, crusty and, finally, charred. The internal temperature of meat continues to rise for a further 10 minutes or so after a high-roasted cut has been taken out of the oven, which is why the resting period is so important and a lot of thought has to be given to timing with this method. It is easier to produce the required doneness when the cooking takes place at a low temperature. Typically this is at 160°C (325°F) Gas 3.

Slow-roasting

Cooking for a long time at a low temperature suits the less tender or drier pieces of meat. It allows the gelatinous, connective tissues time to soften and dissolve, giving a rich, succulent texture and, since there is less shrinkage, the juices are retained inside without much loss of weight. Because this method of cooking leaves the meat with a braised or boiled look, the surface is often browned all over in a pan/skillet on top of the stove first, to give it a roasted appearance. Alternatively, it can be given a quick blast of heat for the last 15 minutes to give the same effect. This meat can be timed to be served either rare or well-done.

Slow roasts benefit from being cooked with vegetables packed around. They supply moisture, absorb meat juices and prevent the roast from drying out. Water, wine or stock is often added as well.

Basting

Basting means to spoon or brush the roast with melted butter, oil, pan juices or stock. It adds flavour and colour and keeps the food from drying out. However fatty roasts, when cooked with the fat side up, such as pork with crackling, do not need to be basted.

A bulb baster (page 16) can also be used for basting, or for drawing fat or juices out of the roasting pan.

When the breast of poultry or the tips of the drumsticks are protected with greased paper or foil, it must be removed from time to time so the skin can be basted to keep it from drying out and becoming leathery.

On or off the bone?

Bones in meat, fish or poultry act as a frame to stop shrinkage during cooking and will give a looser texture when carved. If the meat breaks away from the bone during cooking or has been deboned, it shrinks and becomes close-textured, even tougher. Bones conduct heat, and so a bone-in roast will cook faster than a boneless one. They also contribute flavour to the dish, so even if a roast has been deboned, those bones are often used under the meat, acting as a makeshift rack, and adding their flavour to the pan juices. A boned-out cut will usually have to be tied into shape, producing a much denser cut. A roast with the bones in to provide structure will often be more tender than a boneless one.

Up on a rack

Poultry, such as duck and goose, contain a great deal of fat which melts and is released during cooking. To prevent them from deep-frying in the fat, the birds are sometimes suspended above the roasting pan on a rack or trivet. This also makes it easier to spoon or siphon off the fat as it is rendered (retain it for basting the meat, roasting the vegetables or using on another occasion). Chicken cooked on a rack over liquid acquires a deliciously crisp skin. The liquid may be water, stock or wine, which can then be used to make gravy.

Trussing of poultry

Poultry used to be trussed to make it a tidier shape. These days, birds are less likely to be trussed with the result that the heat can penetrate better, especially to the area between leg and body, the section most at risk of undercooking.

Fish

Fish is best roasted at high temperature, because it does not need long cooking to tenderize it. Keep the skin on the fish to protect the flesh and give extra flavour. Some recipes recommend flashing the skin under the grill/broiler to caramelize it, rather like crackling. Otherwise, the skin may be taken off before serving.

Fish cooked on the bone will have more flavour. Depending on the formality of the occasion, it can be served as is, or taken off the bone for serving. The Chinese have a tradition that it is bad luck to turn the fish over during boning. Bad luck or not, you will find that it keeps its shape better if you serve the top fillets first, then remove the bone (snipping at head and tail with scissors if necessary) before serving the bottom fillets.

Vegetables

Watery vegetables such as squash or tomatoes are best roasted at high temperatures. Vegetables to be roasted until charred to give a grilled effect, such as peppers, courgettes/zucchinis or onions, should be brushed with oil before being subjected to a high temperature and then cooked more slowly until tender.

Root vegetables, especially potatoes and parsnips, may be given a preliminary par-boiling in salted water, to soften the outer surface so that it can become crisp and brown when basted with fat and cooked around the roast. After an initial burst at high temperature, root vegetables, if cooked from raw, rather than par-boiled first, will need further cooking with the temperature lowered to let the heat penetrate to the centre.

fats and oils for roasting

Although most roasts begin their time in the oven with a preliminary brushing with oil, butter, or goose or duck fat, roasting is not in fact a fatty form of cooking. More fat comes out of a roast during cooking than is ever put into it or onto it at the start. The rendered fat is either poured off or taken off with a baster, and only a tablespoon or so used to make a gravy or sauce.

Unfortunately rendered animal fats tend to be high in saturates, but those from poultry, which are liquid at room temperature, have a higher proportion of polyunsaturates and contribute a delicate and delicious taste when combined with other foods or used as a roasting medium (roast potatoes being a prime example).

Oils can be heated to a much higher temperature than boiling water, which is 100°C (212°F). A higher temperature is needed to make the outside layer of food crisp and brown, intensifying its flavour while leaving the inside juicy and moist. Quickly browning meat in a very hot frying pan/skillet before cooking it in a low oven is a well known way of adding a 'roasted' flavour to an otherwise braised piece of meat, since browning can only take place at a high temperature – typically 200°C (400°F).

There is an upper limit to the temperature oils should reach. This varies from oil to oil, but it should not be allowed to reach its 'smoke point'. Not only is the smoke itself obnoxious, but any food in contact with it becomes tainted. Refined safflower and olive oils are among the best for using at high temperatures, because they have high smoke points, whereas butter and other animal fats have lower smoke points. For this reason, clarified butter is often mixed with oil, because it can be heated to a higher temperature. It should be noted that over-using and over-heating any fat or oil causes them to disintegrate and become a health hazard.

Butter

In my opinion, this is the roasting fat par excellence. It is a pure, natural food and gives wonderful flavour to anything it touches. However, it does have a low smoke point and the solids will burn if it gets too hot. These will show as small black spots in the melted butter. They can be avoided by keeping the temperature low, or by using clarified butter (ghee) which has a higher smoke point. I would never choose margarine for cooking or eating.

Goose and duck fat

These highly flavourful cooking fats give extra panache to foods cooked in them, particularly potatoes. The birds give off a great deal of fat while roasting, so there is no need to add more. Keep pouring off or drawing off the fat as the birds roast to stop them stewing in their own oil. In fact, it pays to cook them up on a rack to avoid this problem. Both these fats are prized by cooks and are unlikely to be consumed in enough quantity to pose a health threat. However there are some authorities which suggest that the fat of water birds is one of the healthiest of animal fats, manifested in the phenomenon known as the French Paradox. This suggests that the people of

south-west France, who have a diet high in butter, goose and duck fats (and red wine) have a lower rate of heart disease than other Western populations.

Other animal fats and oils

Before olive oil was widely used in the kitchen – say the 1960s and earlier – dripping from the weekend roast was kept for frying during the week and for starting the roast the following weekend. This practice has now fallen into disuse not only because of theories that animal fats are unhealthy, but also because people are now more likely to use vegetable oils for cooking.

Since red meat fats contain a high proportion of saturated fat, these are not to be recommended on health grounds. However, every type of meat has its own individual flavour concentrated in its fat and from a culinary point of view, there is no way of substituting one animal's fat for another while keeping the original flavour. Gravies are of particular importance in this case and, although fat is often siphoned off or combined with flour before the gravy is made, it is the residual fat which gives much of the characteristic flavour. Fat found marbling through meat is a definite sign of quality because, unless it is a specifically bred characteristic, lean meat tends to come from inadequately or wrongly fed animals and won't be as tender as marbled meat.

Olive oil

If you're going to have only one kind of cooking oil in your larder, make it olive oil. Refined olive oil reaches smoke point at 210°C (410°F), and unrefined at 154°C (310°F).

Peanut oil

Also known as arachide oil or groundnut oil, refined peanut oil is favoured because it can be heated to high temperatures and doesn't have an assertive taste. However cold-pressed peanut oil does have a pronounced flavour. Peanut oil has a high smoke point of 232°C (450°F).

Sunflower and safflower oil

These are both excellent oils, high in polyunsaturates and low in saturated fat, making them a healthier option than saturated fats.

Canola and maize/corn oil

Canola or rapeseed oil and maize/corn oil are popular oils. However, these two crops, together with soy, are those that have received most attention from companies developing GM foods. Many people prefer to avoid them.

Unspecified vegetable oil

This is one category it might be wise to stay away from. It is a combination of various oils, which are always highly refined. It almost always contains palm oils, which are almost as heavy in saturated fats as animal fat.

Saturated fats in general

It is generally accepted that large proportions of saturated fats in the diet are heart and health risks. Saturated fats generally come from animal sources in the form of butter, lard or dripping, but also from coconut oil and palm oil.

Keeping oils

The flavour of fats and oils is one of their most useful attributes, but it is prone to contamination and deterioration. The most usual damage is caused by leaving them open to the air, when they tend to go rancid. Sun also has a deleterious effect, as do moulds and bacteria which are encouraged to increase by moisture left in the fat after food has been cooked in it. So – keep fats and oils in a dark cool place, in a non-reactive, airtight container. However well looked after, they will deteriorate with age and should not be used beyond their use-by date.

Virgin olive oils last about 1 year, ordinary olive oils and other monounsaturates for about 8 months.

utensils

Roasting pans
Buy at least one large pan, large enough to take a turkey, but make sure it isn't too big to fit in your oven. Almost any kind of metal will do, but the thicker it is, the less likely it is to warp. On the other hand, don't buy something so heavy that you can't lift it and the roast out of the oven – a dangerous activity.

Buy at least 2 smaller roasting pans that will fit in your oven side-by-side. Use them for roasting smaller pieces of meat or poultry, or for vegetables and stuffings. Always choose a roasting pan only a little larger than the bird or cut of meat you wish to roast. If the pan is too large, the oils and juices will spread out too much and so burn too easily.

Roasting rack
A roasting rack should fit your roasting pan snugly. If it isn't wide enough or stable enough, you may get your fingers burned as the rack slips towards you. This is particularly true of the kind shaped like half-cylinders.

Racks are used for very fatty roasts, such as goose, duck or some pork dishes, or even for regular roasts when people are concerned about fats in their diets. If you don't have a rack, you can use a bed of vegetables or bones to keep the roast off the bottom of the pan.

Gravy separator
A separator is a clear glass jug/pitcher with a long spout rising from the base, a bit like an exaggerated teapot. Pour the gravy juices into the separator – the fat rises to the top and you can pour off the juices from the bottom via the spout.

Bulb baster
Invaluable for drawing off cooking fats and juices from the tin to baste the roast, or just to remove fat safely. If you don't have one, use a large tablespoon instead.

Thermometers
A meat thermometer is the only accurate way of gauging the inner temperature of a roast. Leave it in for the whole resting period – the maximum temperature is often achieved only after resting.

There are two kinds. One you insert from the beginning of cooking and this one is widely available. The other, the size of a fountain pen, is stuck into the meat when you think it's done and it gives an instant reading. The instant-read kind is available by mail order, in kitchen stores, department stores and hardware stores/general housewares stores. They are very popular with professional chefs, and a wonderful gadget for the home cook.

If a thermometer is unavailable, test chicken and other poultry by inserting a skewer into the thickest part of the thigh. The juices should run clear and golden (press a metal spoon against the thigh to check the colour). If there is any trace of blood, return to the oven and cook longer until the juices are clear. Meats should be timed carefully according to the temperatures and timings given in the chart on page 19.

Oven mitts
Use oven mitts to take pans out of the oven. Never touch hot metal with a wet cloth – the water turns to steam and you can be scalded.

roasting times

Beef

There are two cooking methods to choose from when meat is to be served rare. First, it can be roasted in a very hot oven, then left to rest in a warm place. This allows the juices to redistribute themselves. It must be reheated for about 15–20 minutes in a very hot oven before serving. Alternatively, it can be given the traditional treatment. This involves starting the roasting process in a hot oven 220°C (425°F) Gas 7, then lowering the heat to 180°C (350°F) Gas 4 for the calculated roasting time (page 19). Allow 15 minutes per 500 g/1 lb. for rare meat, 20 minutes per 500 g/1 lb. for a medium roast and 30 minutes per 500 g/1 lb. for well done meat.

Lamb

To obtain a crisp coating for roast lamb, rub the exposed fat with highly seasoned flour. Mix 125 g/¾ cup plain/all-purpose flour with 1 teaspoon salt and ¼ teaspoon coarsely ground black pepper and store in an airtight container. Add herbs just before cooking.

Alternatively, pierce the surface at intervals, insert slivers of garlic and sprigs of rosemary, then brush with olive oil.

Roast in a hot oven 220°C (425°F) Gas 7 for 20 minutes, then at 190°C (375°F) Gas 5 at 20 minutes to every 500 g/1 lb. for the timed period. If it is to be served pink, allow 15 minutes to every 500 g/1 lb.

Pork

This densely textured meat should be served without any trace of pinkness, but at the same time care should be taken not to overcook it or it will become dry and tough. The best method is to slow-roast at 170°C (325°F) Gas 3 without any high starting temperature – this results in a necessarily long cooking time of 40 minutes to every 500 g/1 lb. Season the meat with salt and pepper as well as optional herbs or garlic before cooking.

If the pork still has its rind on, this must be scored before cooking to produce a crisp crackling. The oven temperature must be raised to maximum for the final 20 minutes. Many cooks baste every 8 minutes with the hot pan drippings, though I do not. Let cool a little before carving. Do NOT season crackling before roasting, though it is common practice to do so. Salt draws moisture to the surface and inhibits the skin from making crackling.

Chicken

Before cooking, chicken should be brushed with melted butter or oil to protect its fine skin, then you can protect it further with either strips of bacon or a covering of kitchen foil. Remove for the final 20 minutes and raise the oven temperature to brown the skin. The cavity can be well seasoned before cooking with lemon, tarragon and/or salt.

Duck and goose

Oven-ready and frozen duck are available all year and so are geese, although in spring you are more likely to find these frozen. Duck are usually 3–3.5 kg/5–6 lb., while geese are usually 5–7 kg/10–12 lb. Allow at least 500 g/ 1 lb. per person dressed weight.

Both are water birds and so have darker flesh than chicken or turkey, with a richer

meat – roasting times chart

	starting temperature for 20 minutes	roasting temperature	cooking time – per kg/lb.	instant-read temperature
beef rare	220°C (425°F) Gas 7	170°C (325°F) Gas 3	30/15 minutes	60°C/140°F
medium	220°C (425°F) Gas 7	180°C (350°F) Gas 4	45/20 minutes	65°C/150°F
well done	220°C (425°F) Gas 7	190°C (375°F) Gas 5	65/30 minutes	70°C/160°F
lamb	220°C (425°F) Gas 7	190°C (375°F) Gas 5	45/20 minutes	77°C/170°F
pork	n/a	170°C (325°F) Gas 3	85/40 minutes	80°C/175°F
pork crackling	n/a	final 30 minutes at 250°C (455°F) Gas 9	n/a	n/a
veal	brown in frying pan first	170°C (325°F) Gas 3	65/25 minutes	70°C/160°F
chicken (whole)	n/a	200°C (400°F) Gas 6	45/20 minutes	82°C/180°F
chicken (pieces)	220°C (425°F) Gas 7 for 10 mins	160°C (325°F) Gas 3	total 30 minutes	n/a
duck	220°C (425°F) Gas 7	170°C (325°F) Gas 3	85/40 minutes	82°C/180°F
goose	230°C (450°F) Gas 7	180°C (350°F) Gas 4	40/20 minutes	82°C/180°F
turkey	*see chart on page 21*			82°C/180°F
guinea fowl	n/a	170°C (325°F) Gas 3	total 1½ hours	80°C/175°F
quail	brown in pan/skillet first	230°C (450°F) Gas 8	10 minutes	n/a
pheasant (young)	n/a	200°C (400°F) Gas 6	total 35 minutes	82°C/180°F
rabbit (whole)	n/a	190°C (375°F) Gas 5	total 1 hour	70°C/160°F
rabbit (pieces)	n/a	190°C (375°F) Gas 5	20–30 minutes	n/a
venison	as for beef, depending on cut	200°C (400°F) Gas 6	as for beef, depending on cut	65°C/150°F

textured meat enclosed in a heavy layer of fat to protect them against the elements. This fat is much prized by connoisseurs. It is melted or rendered during cooking, then collected and stored for future use, such as roasting potatoes, moistening sauerkraut or other forms of cabbage and making duck and goose confits.

To prepare these birds for the oven, prick them all over with a sharp-pronged fork, skewer or larding needle, especially on the upper leg near the body. Stand the bird on a trivet or rack so the large amounts of fat can be drained off. This should be done 3–4 times during roasting, both for safety (so it doesn't burn) and to prevent the bird from being deep-fried in its own fat. To start the rendering process, the oven temperature starts high, typically at 220°C (425°F) Gas 7 (duck) and 230°C (450°F) Gas 8 (goose) and is then reduced for the main part of the cooking to 170°C (325°F) Gas 3 (duck) and 180°C (350°F) Gas 4 (goose).

Game
The game listed here is all farmed game. For information on cooking wild game, consult a specialist cookbook. Only young game is roasted, because the flesh is still tender. The oven temperature is kept high throughout the cooking of smaller birds such as quail. Older pheasants may be cooked at a high temperature first, then lowered and cooked for a longer time.

Rabbit is better roasted in pieces rather than whole. The legs should be cooked for slightly longer than other cuts.

Venison should be roasted until just rare, then let rest afterwards. It will continue to cook and, by the time you carve it (after 10 minutes), it will be a uniform brown colour. If you cook it until very rare, then rest it for just 10 minutes, it will carve with a gentle pinkness. It is at its most tender served in this way.

Turkey
A perfectly cooked turkey is brown and crisp on the outside, but juicy without a trace of blood on the inside, especially at its thickest part where the leg joins the body. This means that at the leg joint, the temperature must be 77°C (170°F), the meat juices run clear, and more importantly at this temperature salmonella and other harmful bacteria are rendered harmless.

For this to happen three things must be taken into consideration:

• the weight of the bird

• the oven temperature

• length of time per 500 g/1 lb. used to calculate the overall cooking time.

Weigh the turkey and include in its weight any interior stuffings. Calculate the cooking time using the chart opposite, allowing plenty of time for resting the bird and dishing it up. Check the chart for oven temperatures and roasting times.

The lower the temperature, the longer the bird will take to cook and the juicier it will be. It is possible to cook a turkey overnight and finish it just before serving. However, unless something is done about it, the skin will not be a nice, crisp brown. If the oven temperature is set high, the time per kilo will be less, but there is a likelihood that the meat will not be cooked on the inside before the outside is overdone. So a compromise is called for – this is it. Start high, then turn the oven low for most of the cooking time, then high again (as in the chart below).

If using a frozen turkey, thaw it according to the chart. Do not let turkey liquid drip onto other foods in the refrigerator.

turkey – roasting times chart

Allow 500 g/1 lb. per person. Final internal temperature with an instant-read thermometer: 82°C/180°F

trussed weight	approx. thawing time in refrigerator	time at high temperature 220°C (425°F) Gas 7	time at basic temperature 170°C (335°F) Gas 3	time at finishing temperature 220°C (425°F) Gas 7	total cooking time	resting time
4 kg / 9 lbs	65 hours	20 minutes	140 minutes	30 minutes	190 mins	30 mins
5 kg / 11 lbs	70 hours	25 minutes	165 minutes	30 minutes	220 mins	30 mins
6 kg / 13¼ lbs	75 hours	35 minutes	200 minutes	30 minutes	265 mins	40 mins
7 kg / 15½ lbs	75 hours	40 minutes	230 minutes	30 minutes	300 mins	40 mins
8 kg / 17½ lbs	80 hours	45 minutes	230 minutes	35 minutes	310 mins	50 mins
9 kg / 20 lbs	80 hours	50 minutes	245 minutes	35 minutes	330 mins	60 mins
10 kg / 22 lbs	80 hours	50 minutes	265 minutes	35 minutes	350 mins	60 mins

meat

roast beef with all the trimmings

Only the very best meat should be used for this delicious roast. The art is not so much in the cooking as in the timing, so you don't end up with everybody waiting for you at the table, while you have forgotten to make the gravy.

3 kg/6½ lb. bone-in forerib of beef (2–3 bones)

2 tablespoons plain/all-purpose flour

1 tablespoon hot mustard powder

75 g/3 oz. beef dripping, shortening or 4 tablespoons olive oil

3 onions, quartered

8–10 potatoes, cut into chunks and parboiled

5–6 parsnips, halved lengthways

sea salt and freshly ground black pepper

accompaniments

1 recipe Horseradish Sauce (page 230)

1 recipe Yorkshire Puddings (page 234)

1.25 kg/3 lb. green vegetable, such as cabbage, sliced and steamed or boiled

1 recipe Gravy (page 226)

an instant-read thermometer

serves 8–10

Preheat the oven to 240°C (475°F) Gas 8. Season the meat, mix the flour and the mustard and pat it onto the beef fat. Put the dripping or oil in a roasting pan, put the onions in the middle and set the beef, fat side up, on top. Put the potatoes and parsnips around the meat and put the pan in the preheated oven.

After 20 minutes cooking time, reduce oven heat to 190°C (375°F) Gas 5, baste the beef and turn the vegetables in the fat. Make the horseradish sauce and set aside. Baste the beef and turn the potatoes and parsnips in the fat.

When the roast has been in the oven for an hour and a half, increase the oven temperature to 240°C (475°F) Gas 8 and spoon 4 tablespoons of the fat into a large Yorkshire pudding pan. Heat the fat on the top of the stove and pour the Yorkshire pudding batter into the pan. Put the Yorkshire pudding pan in the oven.

When the beef has been roasting for an hour and 40 minutes, or when a meat thermometer registers 60°C (175°F) (or a little below if you like beef very rare), take the beef out of the oven. Lift the beef onto a serving dish, add the vegetables and set aside in a warm place. It will go on cooking as it rests.

Put the green vegetable on to boil and make the gravy in the roasting pan and pour into a gravy boat. Dish up the green vegetables and keep them warm. Serve the Yorkshire pudding around the beef or on a separate platter. Put the beef on the table with the horseradish sauce and the gravy.

fillet of beef and mushrooms wrapped in parma ham

This cut is the most tender of all and easy to cook – you just roast it to the pinkness you require. However, this can be a bit dull, so some salty, smoky ham and sweet port and mushrooms will give it all the extra flavour it needs. Cooked to this recipe, then let rest, the meat will be a gentle rosy pink all through when it is carved. An added bonus is that it is also delicious served cold with a salad and chutney next day.

30 g/2 tablespoons unsalted butter

1 small onion, chopped

150 g/6 oz. mushrooms, sliced

**2 tablespoons port mixed with
1 tablespoon brandy**

12 slices Parma ham

750 g/1½ lb. fillet of beef

sea salt and freshly ground black pepper

to serve

fresh Horseradish Sauce (page 230)

sautéed potatoes

steamed green beans

an instant-read thermometer

serves 4–6

Melt the butter in a frying pan/skillet, add the onion and cook gently for 5 minutes until softened. Add the mushrooms and cook until they have absorbed all the butter and become softened too, adding more butter if necessary.

Season with salt and pepper, then remove the pan/skillet from the heat to add the port and brandy mixture, letting it sizzle and lose the alcohol before returning it to the stove. Reduce the liquid until it has all been absorbed by the mushrooms. Cool and set aside.

Arrange 6 slices of ham crossways in a roasting pan, overlapping them to fit the length of the meat. Spread the mushroom mixture over the ham to cover it, then season the beef and set it on top. Cover with the remaining ham, tucking the slices under and around so that no beef is visible.

Roast in an oven preheated to 220°C (425°F) Gas 7 for 40 minutes or until an instant-read thermometer registers 60°C (140°F). Turn off the oven and leave the door open. The internal temperature of the meat will continue to rise to 70°C (158°F), at which point it will be an even rosy pink when sliced. Serve with fresh horseradish sauce, sautéed potatoes and steamed green beans.

Note The usual timings given for other cuts of beef do not apply to fillets. This is because they are long and thin, and the heat only need get through this narrow thickness. The timing will be the same, no matter how long the fillet is.

roast beef rib-eye with café de Paris butter and asparagus

Said to have originated in Geneva in the 1940s, you will see many versions of this delicious butter. Great with steak, but also lovely melted on a piece of fish, hot from the grill. Some recipes have a long ingredients list, but essentially it is softened butter combined with curry powder, anchovies, Worchestershire sauce and some fresh herbs.

750–800 g/1¾–2 lb. beef fillet/tenderloin

1 tablespoon sea salt

½ teaspoon freshly ground black pepper

1 tablespoon olive oil

a bunch of white asparagus, trimmed and halved

a bunch of green asparagus, trimmed and halved

2 tablespoons butter

café de Paris butter

1 tablespoon mild mustard

2 teaspoons Worcestershire sauce

3 tablespoons tomato purée/paste

1 teaspoon mild curry powder

1 tablespoon finely chopped shallots

1 garlic clove, crushed

1 tablespoon salted capers, rinsed, well drained and chopped

6 anchovy fillets in olive oil, drained and finely chopped

2 tablespoons chopped fresh parsley

1 teaspoon fresh thyme leaves

115 g/1 stick unsalted butter, softened

serves 4

To make the café de Paris butter, put all of the ingredients in a food processor and process until well combined. Lay a piece of clingfilm/plastic wrap on a work surface. Spoon the butter down the centre, then roll up firmly to make a log. The butter can be made 1–2 days in advance and refrigerated until needed. It should be removed from the refrigerator 1 hour before you plan to serve the beef.

Remove the beef from the refrigerator 1 hour before cooking and rub it all over with the salt and pepper.

Preheat the oven to 220°C (425°F) Gas 7.

Set the roasting pan over high heat. Add the oil to the pan and heat until very hot. Add the beef and cook for 4 minutes, turning every minute, until it is well browned all over. Transfer the roasting pan to the preheated oven and cook for 10 minutes. Turn the beef over and cook for a further 5 minutes. Remove the beef from the oven and sit it on a large sheet of foil. Pour over any pan juices and lightly wrap up in the foil. Let rest in a warm place for 15–20 minutes.

Bring a saucepan of lightly salted water to the boil. Add the asparagus and cook for 1 minute. Drain well. Heat the butter in a frying pan set over high heat. Add the asparagus, season well with salt and pepper and stir-fry for 3–4 minutes, until just wilting and lightly golden.

Serve thick slices of the beef with a few slices of café de Paris butter on top. Arrange the asparagus alongside.

roast boned beef loin basted with wine gravy

This cut of beef is often prepared by a butcher ready to be sliced into steaks, but it can be bought in a whole piece and is the easiest cut to carve. The meat is very tender and except, for the outside, is free from fat.

1.5 kg/3 lb. strip loin of beef (boned sirloin, without the undercut)

3 garlic cloves, sliced

6 small tip sprigs of thyme

100 g/1 stick unsalted butter

2 onions, sliced

125 ml/½ cup red wine

sea salt and coarsely ground black pepper

an instant-read thermometer

serves 6

Trim off a sheet of fat from the top of the meat and keep it to use as a cushion under the roast. Make 6 slits in the underside of the meat and push in a sliver of garlic and a sprig of thyme. Season with the salt and pepper and spread half the butter generously over the underside of the meat. Set the fat in a roasting pan and put the sliced onions on top. Add the sirloin and roast in a preheated oven at 220°C (425°F) Gas 7 for 20 minutes.

Pour the wine into the pan, let it bubble for a moment, then spoon it over the beef. Continue to cook the meat until it is done to your liking, preferably pink, or when an instant-read thermometer registers 65°C (150°F). Baste the meat frequently, adding water to the pan when the wine becomes low.

Transfer the meat to a carving platter and let it rest in a warm place for 10 minutes.

To make a light gravy, add 25 ml/2 tablespoons water to the roasting pan and stir it through the reduced wine. Stir in the remaining butter to make a sauce. Strain into a saucepan, bring to the boil, then add salt and pepper to taste. Serve in a separate sauceboat.

roast fillet of beef with soy and butter sauce

The soy and butter sauce may sound unconventional, but it makes a very light, savoury, meaty sauce. Delicious served with roast new potatoes and green beans.

1 teaspoon coarse sea salt

2 teaspoons black peppercorns

½ teaspoon ground allspice

1 tablespoon plain/all-purpose flour

1 kg/2¼ lb. fillet of beef

1 tablespoon sunflower/safflower or light olive oil

40 g/3 tablespoons soft butter

2 tablespoons Madeira or dry Marsala

375 ml/1½ cups fresh beef stock or stock made with ¾ organic, low-salt beef stock/bouillon cube

1½ tablespoons Japanese soy sauce, such as Kikkoman

serves 6

Preheat the oven to 225°C (425°F) Gas 7.

Put the coarse salt and peppercorns in a mortar and grind with a pestle until finely ground. Mix in the allspice and flour. Remove any fat or sinew from the beef fillet and dry thoroughly with paper towels. Put the seasoning and flour on a plate and roll the beef in the mixture, patting it evenly into the surface and shaking off any excess. Put a casserole or roasting pan over medium to high heat, add the oil and half the butter and brown the beef quickly on all sides. Transfer to the preheated oven and roast for 20–40 minutes, depending how thick your beef fillet is and how rare you like it. Remove from the oven and set aside for 10–15 minutes, lightly covered with foil. Pour off any excess fat in the pan, leaving about 1 tablespoon. Pour in the Madeira and let it bubble up for a few seconds, then add the stock and soy sauce. Bring to the boil, turn the heat down a little and reduce by half. Pour any juices that have accumulated under the meat into the pan, whisk in the remaining butter and season with black pepper (you shouldn't need any salt).

Carve the meat into thick slices and serve on warmed plates with the sauce spooned over and served with some roast new potatoes and green beans.

braised pot roast with red wine, rosemary and bay leaves

This is the sort of food that makes you long for cold wintry days, when it is nice to stay indoors and simmer something slowly – heating the kitchen and filling the house with rich, warming aromas. It also has appeal for the lazy spendthrift as preparation is minimal and the cut of meat is inexpensive. There are several nice accompaniments for this: you could serve creamy mashed potatoes, soft polenta or even macaroni baked in cream with plenty of Parmesan.

1.2 kg/3 lb. braising joint, such as beef brisket, tied

2 tablespoons olive oil

1 onion, halved and thinly sliced

2 celery stalks, thinly sliced

1 large carrot, thinly sliced and cut into half-moons

4 garlic cloves, peeled and sliced

150 g/6 oz. pancetta, very finely chopped

750-ml bottle robust red wine, preferably Italian

400-g/14-oz. can chopped tomatoes

1 bay leaf, 2 large sprigs fresh rosemary, several sprigs fresh parsley, all firmly tied together in a bundle

3–4 tablespoons capers in brine, drained (optional)

sea salt and freshly ground black pepper

serves 6

Preheat the oven to 180°C (350°F) Gas 4.

Heat the oil in a large flameproof casserole. Add the beef and cook for about 8–10 minutes, until browned on all sides. Transfer the beef to a plate, season all over with salt and set aside.

Add the onion, celery and carrot to the casserole and cook, stirring often, until browned. Add the garlic and pancetta and cook for 1 minute. Season, then add the wine and tomatoes and bring to the boil. Continue to boil for 1 minute, then add the herb bundle. Return the browned beef to the casserole.

Cover and transfer to the preheated oven. After 1½ hours, remove the casserole from the oven and turn the beef over. Pour in some water if the liquid has reduced too much and add the capers, if using. Return to the oven and cook for a further 1½ hours, until the meat is tender.

Serve in slices with the sauce and vegetables spooned over the top and with the accompaniment of your choice.

roast stuffed topside with mustard and green peppercorns

This delicious fat-free cut of beef is not the tenderest piece for roasting, but it has a great deal of flavour. Cook it slowly for most of the time, then turn the heat up at the end to give it a good roasting flavour. The meat is cut in two places to make pockets for the stuffing. It produces both rare and medium meat, so all tastes are catered for.

1.5 kg/3¼ lb. beef topside/rump roast

sea salt and freshly ground black pepper

stuffing

60 g/⅓ cup (about 2¼ oz.) cream cheese

1 teaspoon Dijon mustard

1 teaspoon green peppercorns preserved in brine, or coarsely ground black pepper

6 Swiss chard leaves

gravy

1 teaspoon plain/all-purpose flour

250 ml/1 cup beef stock

an instant-read thermometer

serves 4

Cut the meat one-third of the way through its thickness, leaving it attached on one side. Turn the meat over and make another cut one-third of the way down, again leaving it attached on one side, producing 3 thick layers of meat in a Z-shape. Using a sharp knife, carefully remove any gristle that you come across. Season the meat well.

To make the stuffing, put the cream cheese, mustard and peppercorns in a bowl and mash with a fork. Spread the mixture evenly between the layers, adding chard leaves to each layer. Tie up the meat with string to keep the stuffing inside.

Put the meat in a roasting pan and cook in a preheated oven at 250°C (500°F) Gas 9 for 10 minutes. Reduce the temperature to 180°C (350°F) Gas 4 and continue cooking until an instant-read thermometer registers 50°C (120°F) internal temperature.

Finally, increase the temperature to 250°C (500°F) Gas 9 again to crisp up the surface, and when the thermometer registers 65°C (150°F), remove the meat from the oven and transfer to a serving platter. Let rest for 20 minutes.

To make the gravy, pour off all but 1 tablespoon of fat from the roasting pan and put the pan over medium heat on top of the stove. Add the flour and stir into the fat to make a roux. Pour in the stock and bring to the boil, whisking constantly.

Carve the meat thickly, then serve with the gravy.

pot roast brisket with Zinfandel

Brisket is a much underrated cut with a rich flavour. You can use any full-bodied red, but Zinfandel has just the right gutsy rustic character.

200 ml/¾ cup Zinfandel or other full-bodied red wine

200 ml/¾ cup fresh beef stock or stock made with ½ a stock/bouillon cube, cooled

2 tablespoons red wine vinegar

1 large garlic clove, crushed

1 bay leaf

1 onion, chopped

a few of sprigs of thyme or ½ teaspoon dried thyme

1.5 kg/3¼ lb. boned, rolled brisket of beef

2–3 tablespoons sunflower or light olive oil

2 tablespoons dry Marsala or Madeira

sea salt and freshly ground pepper

serves 6

Mix the wine and stock with the wine vinegar, garlic, bay leaf, onion and thyme. Put the meat in a sturdy plastic bag, pour over the marinade and pull the top of the bag together tightly so that the liquid covers the meat. Knot the top of the bag or seal with a wire tie. Leave the meat to marinate in the fridge for at least 4 hours or overnight.

Preheat the oven to 200°C (400°F) Gas 6. Remove the meat from the marinade and dry thoroughly with paper towels. Strain the marinade and reserve the liquid. Heat the oil in a flameproof casserole. Brown the meat all over in the hot oil then add 3–4 tablespoons of the strained marinade. Put a lid on the casserole and roast for 2 hours. Check from time to time that the pan juices are not burning. Add more marinade if necessary, but the flavour of this dish comes from the well-browned sticky juices, so do not add too much extra liquid. If on the other hand more liquid has formed, spoon some out. Simmer the remaining marinade over low heat until it loses its raw, winey taste.

Once the meat is cooked, set it aside in a warm place. Spoon any fat off the surface of the pan juices and add the Marsala and the cooked marinade. Bring to the boil, scraping off all the brown tasty bits from the side of the casserole and adding a little extra water if necessary. Season to taste with salt and pepper and serve spooned over slices of the meat or in a gravy boat for pouring.

french-carved rib steak

A quick and simple way to entertain is to blast a boned piece of tender rib in the oven. Top-quality meat from a small steer is a vital factor in the success of this dish. Gristle or loose texture from a lesser-quality animal would make it tougher and more difficult to carve.

single first rib of the sirloin, boned/
boneless rib steak or rib-eye (about
1½ inches thick)

sea salt flakes

seasoning

2 tablespoons olive oil

2 garlic cloves, crushed

2 teaspoons Dijon mustard

sea salt and coarsely ground black pepper

to serve cold (optional)

crusty bread

rocket/arugula leaves

fresh Horseradish Sauce (page 230)

serves 2

To make the seasoning mixture, put the olive oil, garlic, mustard, salt and pepper in a bowl and mix well. Spread half the seasoning on the upper side of the meat. Put the meat on a rack in a roasting pan and cook in a preheated oven at 250°C (500°F) Gas 9 or maximum for 5 minutes.

Turn the meat over, spread with the rest of the seasoning and cook for a further 5 minutes or less, according to the required state of 'doneness'. Crunch over some sea salt before serving, carved in thick diagonal slices.

You can also serve this cold next day, with crusty bread, rocket/arugula and horseradish.

slow-roasted breast of veal

Roasting a breast of veal is similar to cooking a piece of beef brisket, but the taste is very different and it takes less time. The preliminary browning is done over high heat on top of the stove, then the meat is transferred to the oven for gentle roasting. Wine, garlic and rosemary turn this into a classic Italian favourite.

60 g/4 tablespoons unsalted butter

2 tablespoons olive oil

2 onions, cut into chunks

6 celery stalks, cut into 2½-cm/1-inch lengths

1.5 kg/3¼ lb. breast of veal, on the bone

2–3 sprigs of rosemary

200 ml/¾ cup white wine

3 garlic cloves, crushed with a knife

1 teaspoon tomato purée/paste

sea salt and freshly ground black pepper

serves 4

Put the butter and oil in a heavy frying pan/skillet and set over high heat. When the butter begins to colour, add the onions and celery, turn them over in the fat and fry them until they colour a little. Lower the heat so the butter doesn't burn. This will take about 10 minutes. Spoon them into a roasting pan.

Put the seasoned meat bone side up in the frying pan and brown it well. Turn it over, add the rosemary and brown the underside lightly.

Lift the meat into the roasting pan and transfer to a preheated oven at 170°C (325°F) Gas 3. Add the wine, garlic and tomato purée/paste to the frying pan/skillet. Bring to the boil, then simmer the liquid until it is reduced and syrupy. Add 200 ml/¾ cups water, bring to the boil, then pour it and all the bits in the pan into the roasting pan. Roast the meat, basting it from time to time until tender, usually about 2 hours. You may need to top up with water from time to time to keep the vegetables moist.

Lift the veal onto a carving platter and either cut the meat into thick slices between the bones or, using a sharp knife, remove the bones, which should slide out quite easily. You can then carve the meat into thinner slices. Serve the vegetables with the meat.

Tuscan-style roast veal with wild mushrooms

This delicious Tuscan dish, light but intensely flavourful, is the perfect summer roast served with new potatoes and buttered spinach.

1 kg/1¼ lb. boned, rolled loin or rack of veal or pork (ask the butcher to give you the bones)

3 tablespoons olive oil

50 g/3 tablespoons butter

1 onion, cut into 8

1 large carrot, cut into chunks

3 large garlic cloves, peeled and quartered

3 sprigs of rosemary

250 ml/1 cup dry Italian white wine

250 ml/1 cup fresh chicken stock or light vegetable stock made with ½ organic stock/bouillon cube

150 g/6 oz. wild mushrooms

2 teaspoons plain/all-purpose flour

a few drops of Marsala or sweet sherry (optional)

sea salt and freshly ground black pepper

serves 6

Preheat the oven to 200°C (400°F) Gas 6. Pat the veal dry and season with salt and pepper. Put a casserole over medium heat, add 1½ tablespoons of the olive oil, heat for a minute, then add 1 tablespoon of the butter. When the foaming dies down, put in the veal, bones, onion and carrot and brown on all sides, turning regularly.

Add the garlic and rosemary to the casserole, stir and add 3 tablespoons of the white wine. Cover with a lid and transfer to the oven. Roast for about 2 hours. Check occasionally that the meat and vegetables aren't burning and add a little more white wine if necessary.

Remove the veal from the casserole and set aside on a warmed carving plate. Cover lightly with foil and leave to rest for at least half an hour.

Pour off any surface fat from the juices in the casserole, then add the remaining white wine and bring to the boil, working in the tasty caramelized juices stuck on the side of the casserole. Simmer and reduce the liquid by half, then add half the stock and simmer for another 10 minutes. Strain through a fine sieve/strainer.

Heat the remaining butter in a small frying pan/skillet and fry the mushrooms until the butter and any liquid have almost evaporated. Stir in the flour. Pour in the strained stock, bring to the boil and simmer for 5 minutes. Add a little more stock if the sauce seems too thick. Check the seasoning, add salt and pepper to taste and a dash of Marsala if you like a touch of sweetness.

For a rack of veal, offer the sauce separately, otherwise finely slice the meat, arrange on a warmed platter and spoon over the sauce.

veal with mustard cream

The delicate flavour of veal with cream or cheese is a popular combination. Sour cream is different in different countries. In Eastern and Central Europe – and Australia – it is thick and delicious, a little like mascarpone, and can be used straight on the veal. It reduces to become a dill-flavoured cheese coating on the meat. In other parts of the world, the cream needs some extra preparation. Serve this rich and delicate dish with a peppery watercress salad (and potatoes of course).

1.5 kg/3¼ lb. piece of veal (cushion or topside/boneless loin or rib roast)

2 tablespoons melted butter or olive oil

sea salt and freshly ground black pepper

sour cream crust

75 ml/⅓ cup sour cream

75 ml/⅓ cup double/heavy cream, plus 2 tablespoons extra for the gravy (optional)

1 teaspoon Dijon mustard

1 tablespoon lemon juice

2 tablespoons chopped fresh dill

an instant-read thermometer

serves 6

Put the sour cream, double/heavy cream, mustard and 1 teaspoon of the lemon juice in a bowl and mix well.

Season the meat well with salt and pepper and brush it all over with the melted butter or oil. Set the meat on a sheet of foil and coat it with the dill, patting it on to make it cling.

Smother the meat with the sour cream mixture and pull up the edges of the foil to partly cover the meat, leaving the top exposed. Pour in any remaining melted butter and the remaining lemon juice. Put the parcel in a roasting pan, and transfer to a preheated oven at 170°C (325°F) Gas 3. After about 1 hour, lift out the pan and open the foil to expose the juices that have collected at the bottom. Baste the meat with the juices (but avoid the crust which is forming on the top) and add 1 tablespoon water to the juices if there are not enough to moisten the meat.

Return the meat to the oven for a further 30 minutes and if the crust has not browned, raise the oven temperature to 200°C (400°F) Gas 6 for 15 minutes, or until an instant-read thermometer registers 71°C (160°F).

Lift the veal onto a large platter and drain the juices from the roasting pan into a saucepan. Add the 2 tablespoons cream, reheat gently and serve separately for guests to help themselves.

meatloaf

A meatloaf can make a nice change to a traditional joint, but still goes perfectly with all the traditional roast trimmings. And any (perhaps unlikely) leftovers make the perfect sandwich filling.

1 onion, coarsely chopped

2 garlic cloves

1 celery stalk, coarsely chopped

leaves from a small bunch of fresh parsley

2 tablespoons olive oil

750 g/1 lb. beef mince

350 g/12 oz. pork mince

2 eggs, beaten

2 tablespoons milk

100 g/1 cup fresh breadcrumbs (see note)

1 teaspoon dried thyme

2 teaspoons salt

½ teaspoon ground white pepper

1 teaspoon paprika

60 ml/¼ cup chilli sauce or ketchup

2–3 bay leaves, plus extra to garnish

5–6 streaky/fatty bacon slices

sea salt and freshly ground black pepper

serves 6–8

Preheat the oven to 180°C (350°F) Gas 4.

Combine the onion, garlic, celery and parsley in a food processor and pulse until minced.

Transfer the mixture to a frying pan/skillet, add the oil and cook over low heat for 5–7 minutes, until soft. Transfer to a large bowl and add the beef, pork, eggs, milk, breadcrumbs, thyme, salt, pepper, paprika and chilli sauce. Mix well with your hands until well blended.

Form the mixture into an oval loaf shape, as if you were making bread. Put the bay leaves in the middle of the tray and place the meatloaf on top. Arrange the bacon slices on top, at equal intervals.

Bake in the preheated oven for about 1½ hours, until browned and cooked through. Do check the meatloaf regularly and baste with the pan juices to keep it moist. Serve with mashed potatoes and gravy.

Note The best way to obtain fresh breadcrumbs is to use the end pieces from a sliced loaf, wholemeal or white but nothing with seeds. Simply tear into smaller pieces and put in the bowl of a food processor and processor to obtain crumbs. (The food processor is required for the onions in this recipe as well but do the breadcrumbs first because they are a dry ingredient.)

crunchy roast pork with baked stuffed apples

The combination of pork and apple is a classic one, but it's given a twist in this recipe by stuffing the apples with onion and fresh sage.

1.5-kg/3½-lb. loin of pork, boned and rolled

3 eating apples

1 onion, chopped

8 sage leaves, chopped

1 tablespoon olive oil

sea salt and freshly ground black pepper

gravy

2 tablespoons plain/all-purpose flour

200 ml/1 cup white wine

200 ml/1 cup vegetable stock

sea salt and freshly ground black pepper

serves 6

Preheat the oven to 220°C (425°F) Gas 7, then lightly oil a roasting pan.

Dry the loin of pork with paper towels, place in the prepared pan and roast for 30 minutes. Reduce the heat to 180°C (350°F) Gas 4 and cook the pork for a further 30 minutes.

Slice the apples in half across the middle and cut out the core. Mix the onion and sage with the oil and season. Arrange the apple halves around the roasting pork and fill the cavities with the stuffing. Return to the oven and cook for 30 minutes. When cooked, transfer the pork and apples to a carving plate and keep warm.

To make the gravy, drain half the fat from the roasting pan, add the flour and mix until smooth. Pour in the wine and stock and mix thoroughly. Place the roasting pan directly over the heat and keep stirring until the gravy thickens. Adjust the seasoning. For a very smooth gravy, press it through a sieve. Serve the pork with the roast apples, a selection of vegetables and the gravy.

slow-roasted pork loin with rosemary, madeira and orange

Without crackling to add texture, pork cries out for some form of flavouring – the loin is the ideal cut for such treatment. Ask your butcher to chine it by removing the backbone, or to cut it down between the ribs, so that you can carve it easily into cutlets. This is a very dense meat, so gentle roasting is the only way to prevent it drying out, giving ample time for the full flavour to develop.

1.5 kg/3 lb. centre loin of pork

200 ml/1 cup Madeira wine

100 ml/½ cup freshly squeezed orange juice

2 sprigs of rosemary, bruised

2 oranges, peeled and sliced into 4 slices each

sea salt and freshly ground black pepper

an instant-read thermometer

serves 4

Score the fat with a criss cross pattern and season the meat with plenty of salt and pepper, rubbing it in well. Put a double thickness of kitchen foil in a large roasting pan and turn up the edges. Put in the meat fat side down and pour in the Madeira and juice. Add the rosemary. Leave for about 2 hours if possible, then put in the middle of a preheated oven at 170°C (325°F) Gas 3 and slow-roast for 1 hour.

Carefully turn the meat over, then add the orange slices and about 125 ml/½ cup water if it is starting to dry out. Cook for a further 30 minutes. Then raise the oven temperature to 220°C (425°F) Gas 7 for a final 10 minutes or until an instant-read thermometer registers 80°C (175°F).

Lift the meat out onto a serving dish and arrange the orange slices around. Carefully pour the juices into a jug/pitcher, then serve.

slow-cooked spiced pork belly with apple and fennel

Look out for pork belly at the farmer's market or a specialty butcher. You could also roast a shoulder or leg joint of pork for this recipe. You can't go far wrong with this low-temperature, slow-cooking method, which produces crispy skin and melt-in-the-mouth meat. This is great for dinner parties – it greets your guests with a delicious aroma, creating a mood of anticipation, which is the key to good entertaining.

1 tablespoon fennel seeds

2 teaspoons caraway seeds

4 garlic cloves

2 tablespoons olive oil

1 kg/2¼ lbs. pork belly, picnic shoulder or Boston butt

4 apples, such as Cox's Orange Pippin

2 fennel bulbs, with feathery tops intact, cut into thick wedges

sea salt and freshly ground black pepper

serves 4

Combine the fennel and caraway seeds, garlic and 1 tablespoon salt in a mortar and pound with a pestle. Stir in 1 tablespoon of the olive oil.

Cut ½-cm/¼-inch deep incisions, spaced 1–2 cm/about ½ inch apart, across the skin of the pork. Rub the spice mixture into the incisions, and let sit for 1 hour at cool room temperature.

Preheat the oven to 140°C (275°F) Gas 1.

Put the pork in a large roasting pan and cook in the preheated oven for 3 hours in total. (You'll need to remove the pan from the oven 30 minutes before the end of the cooking time to add the apples and fennel.)

Put the remaining oil in a large bowl and season with a little salt and pepper. Add the apples and the fennel bulbs with feathery tops to the bowl and use your hands to toss until evenly coated in oil. Thirty minutes before the end of the cooking time, remove the pork from the oven and arrange the apples and fennel in the tin. Increase the heat to 220°C (425°F) Gas 7 and return the tin to the oven.

Remove the pork from the oven, cover loosely with foil and let rest for about 20 minutes. Carve into slices and serve with the roasted apples and fennel on the side.

spiced roast ham or pork with juniper berries

This dish is for Christmas time – the spices lightly pickle the meat and give it an intriguing Eastern flavour. They must be rubbed in dry so the flavours penetrate the meat, then later the oil is added to moisten it. Because there is a great deal of fatless meat on a ham, it will dry out and toughen unless basted frequently. If you are using the trotter end of a half leg, wrap it with a thick collar of foil during the later part of the cooking to keep it moist. The meat taken from the top end of the leg may be tunnel-boned for easier carving. It is delicious cold.

½ leg of pork or ham, about 2.5 kg/5 lb.

2–3 tablespoons peanut or sunflower/safflower oil

275 ml/1¼ cups water or chicken stock

sea salt

spice mixture

1 teaspoon ground coriander

1 teaspoon ground cumin

1 teaspoon ground caraway

1 teaspoon ground ginger

½ teaspoon ground cinnamon

½ teaspoon ground allspice

½ teaspoon freshly grated nutmeg

12 juniper berries, crushed

an instant-read thermometer

serves 6

To prepare the spice mixture, put the coriander, cumin, caraway, ginger, cinnamon, allspice, nutmeg and juniper berries in a bowl and mix well. Remove the rind from the meat and rub the dry spices into all the crevices in the meat. Wrap it in clingfilm/plastic wrap or a plastic bag and refrigerate for 48 hours.

Score the fat with a criss cross pattern on the upper side of the meat. Put in a roasting pan, baste with the oil and sprinkle well with salt. Put the pan in the middle of a preheated oven at 240°C (475°F) Gas 8 and add 5–6 tablespoons water. Roast for 10 minutes, then reduce the temperature to 170°C (325°F) Gas 3 and cook for 2½ hours. Baste from time to time and add extra water as necessary to keep it moist because this will form the base of the gravy.

When an instant-read thermometer reaches 80°C (175°F), transfer the meat to a serving dish and let it rest for 10 minutes.

Meanwhile, deglaze the pan with the water or stock to make a gravy, then boil to reduce and intensify the flavours. Taste and, if necessary, adjust the seasoning with salt. Carve the meat in thin slices and serve the gravy separately in a jug/pitcher.

rolled pork roast with sage and onion stuffing

This is an ideal cut of pork for serving with crackling: it is tender and moist and will stand the high temperature at the end of the cooking time needed to produce the crunch. Even if you can't get the meat with its outer skin still on, it is still delicious when boned and stuffed with the sage and onion filling. If you don't have the rind on the meat, miss out the final high roasting part at the end.

2 kg/4 lb. blade or hand of pork/pork arm roast or Boston butt, with rind if possible, and scored

1 teaspoon sea salt

2 tablespoons olive oil, for brushing

stuffing

1 onion, finely chopped

1 green apple, such as Granny Smith, cut into small pieces

2 celery stalks, finely chopped

60 g/½ cup cashew nuts, chopped

50 g/4 tablespoons unsalted butter

2 teaspoons chopped fresh sage leaves

grated zest and freshly squeezed juice of 1 unwaxed lemon

250 g/3 cups fresh breadcrumbs

cider gravy

125 ml/½ cup cider vinegar

250 ml/1 cup water or chicken stock

an instant-read thermometer

serves 6

To make the stuffing, put the onion, apple, celery, cashews, butter, sage, lemon zest and juice and breadcrumbs in a bowl. Mix well.

Season the inside of the pork with the salt, then spread the stuffing over that side, roll up the meat and tie it with string to make a good shape. Brush with the oil and set it on a rack in a roasting pan. Add 250 ml/1 cup water. Put it in a cold oven, turn the heat to 220°C (425°F) Gas 7 and roast for 30 minutes.

Reduce the oven temperature to 170°C (325°F) Gas 3. Cook for another 1½ hours or until an instant-read thermometer registers 80°C (175°F). Transfer the meat to another roasting pan or a baking sheet with sides. Do not baste during this time.

Raise the oven temperature to maximum and return the meat to the very hot oven for another 20 minutes to crisp the surface.

Meanwhile, make the gravy by deglazing the roasting pan with the vinegar and reducing it well. Add the water or stock, bring to the boil, then taste and adjust the seasoning with salt if necessary. Serve in a sauceboat.

When the crackling on the meat is ready, transfer the roast to a carving platter and let rest for 10–20 minutes before carving in fairly thick slices.

roast pork fillets with creamy Thai-spiced sauce

This is every aspiring cook's favourite cut of meat, but unfortunately it is also one that can be overcooked only too easily. This is especially true if the meat is cut into medallions, so cook it as a whole piece, as here, and cut it into medallions later. Serve with mashed potatoes or stir-fried vegetables.

2 pork fillets/tenderloins, 500 g/1 lb. each, trimmed

6 spring onion/scallion tops, thickly sliced diagonally

mashed potatoes or stir-fried vegetables, to serve

vinaigrette marinade

4 tablespoons/¼ cup rice vinegar

4 tablespoons/¼ cup olive oil

½ teaspoon salt

½ teaspoon Thai seven-spice

creamy Thai-spiced sauce

3 cm/1 inch piece fresh ginger, grated

2 tablespoons cider vinegar

4 tablespoons/½ cup sweet sherry

1 tablespoon peanut or sunflower/safflower oil

250 ml/1 cup coconut milk

1 teaspoon sugar

½ teaspoon Thai seven-spice

a pinch of salt, to taste

serves 6

To make a vinaigrette marinade, put the rice vinegar, olive oil, salt and seven-spice in shallow dish, mix well, then add the fillets. Turn to coat with the marinade mixture and set aside for at least 1 hour to marinate.

Put the fillets/tenderloins side by side in a roasting pan, baste them with the marinade and cook in a preheated oven at 250°C (500°F) Gas 9 for 15 minutes, baste again, then roast for a further 15 minutes. Transfer them to a warm place and cover with kitchen foil.

To make the sauce, put the ginger, vinegar, sherry and oil in a small saucepan, heat to simmering and reduce to a syrup. Add the coconut milk, sugar and seven-spice and reduce again to about 125 ml/½ cup or to taste. Taste and adjust the seasoning.

Just before serving, slice the meat into medallions and pour any juice into the sauce. Serve on heated dinner plates. Spoon the sauce over the top and sprinkle with the spring onions/scallions. Serve with mashed potatoes or stir-fried vegetables.

loin of pork with a herb crust

Sometimes this cut is sold without the skin, so it is a good idea to wrap strips of bacon around the meat. The idea is to release some gelatine into the wine to emulsify and combine all the ingredients when you make the gravy. Half a teaspoon of dissolved gelatine added at the end has the same effect, though not the same flavour. Old-fashioned the recipe may be, but it is a classic and still a favourite.

1.5 kg/3 lb. loin of pork, chined and trimmed

pork rind or 6–7 unsmoked streaky/fatty bacon slices (optional)

2 garlic cloves, 1 cut into slivers, 1 crushed

150 ml/⅔ cup red wine

2 tablespoons olive or sunflower/safflower oil

60 g/1⅓ cups fresh breadcrumbs

2 teaspoons chopped fresh thyme

1 tablespoon chopped fresh flat leaf parsley

250 ml/1 cup beef stock

¼ teaspoon powdered gelatine

2 teaspoons redcurrant or cranberry jelly

sea salt and freshly ground black pepper

accompaniments

mashed potatoes

Fennel Roasted in Butter (page 182)

an instant-read thermometer

serves 4

Remove the rind if it is still on the pork and put the rind skin side down in a roasting pan. Alternatively, use unsmoked streaky/fatty bacon or omit altogether. Make several small incisions on the underside of the meat and insert the slivers of garlic (use more if you like). Season the meat with salt and pepper.

Pour the wine into a plastic bag, add 1 tablespoon of the oil, half the thyme, salt, then finally add the meat. Close the bag, excluding as much air as possible and put in a dish in the refrigerator for at least 2 hours.

Preheat the oven to 250°C (500°F) Gas 9, put the meat on top of the rind or bacon in a roasting pan, then lower the heat to 180°C (350°F) Gas 4. Baste with the marinade.

Meanwhile, heat the remaining oil in a pan and add the crushed garlic. When it begins to colour, add the breadcrumbs, the parsley and remaining thyme. Mix to absorb all the oil.

After 1 hour, remove the meat from the oven and pack the seasoned crumbs on top. Don't worry if some fall into the roasting pan – they will act as a gravy thickener later. Baste carefully with the pan juices.

Return the pan to the oven and cook for a further 40 minutes or until an instant-read thermometer registers 80°C (175°F). Lift the meat onto a platter and pour the stock into the pan. Bring to the boil on the top of the stove and, if you're not using pork rind, add the gelatine. Add salt and pepper to taste and melt in the jelly. Serve separately in a jug/pitcher.

roasted pork with apple and fennel puddings

They may sound unusual but these savoury puddings packed with vegetables and honey-sweet raisins make a wonderful alternative to roast vegetables.

1.5 kg/3½ lb. piece of pork loin, skin on

2 tablespoons white wine vinegar

1 tablespoon sea salt

apple and fennel puddings:

3 tablespoons butter

1 onion, chopped

1 celery stalk, thinly sliced

1 green apple, grated

1 fennel bulb, grated

100 g/1 cup fresh breadcrumbs

60 g/⅓ cup raisins

1 egg, lightly beaten

250 ml/1 cup chicken stock

45 g/⅓ cup flaked almonds

serves 6

Make small incisions on the skin of the pork, 1 cm/½-inch apart but don't cut through to the meat. Rub the vinegar and sea salt into the skin and set aside for 1 hour at room temperature. (This will let the skin dry out making for better crackling.)

Preheat the oven to 220°C (425°F) Gas 7. Put the pork on a cooking rack over a roasting pan. Pour 250 ml/1 cup water into the pan and cook in the preheated oven for 30 minutes. Reduce the oven temperature to 180°C (350°F) Gas 4 and cook for a further 1½ hours, until the pork skin is golden and crisp. Keep adding water to the roasting tin during the cooking time as necessary. Remove the pork from the oven, cover with aluminium foil and let rest for 10 minutes.

Meanwhile, make the puddings. Heat the butter in a frying pan over medium heat. When the butter is sizzling, add the onion and celery and cook for 4–5 minutes, stirring often. Add the apple and fennel and cook for 1 minute, stirring well. Remove the pan from the heat and add all the remaining ingredients, except for the almonds. Stir well. Spoon the mixture into the baking dish, sprinkle the almonds on top and cook in a preheated oven at 180°C (350°F) Gas 4 for 1 hour. Serve slices of the pork with wedges of the pudding.

marinated pork roast

If you thought pork was bland, think again. It is actually a spectacular vehicle for all sorts of flavours, and responds remarkably well to marinating. Any cut of pork can be marinated, from a few hours to overnight, and the leftovers are as good, if not better, than the original. Serve with something creamy, like Cauliflower Gratin (page 208), or roasted vegetables.

1 bottle dry white wine, 750 ml

500 ml/2 cups white wine vinegar

1 large onion, sliced

2 carrots, sliced

1 fresh bay leaf

a sprig of thyme

1 celery stalk, with leaves

2 garlic cloves, sliced

1 teaspoon peppercorns

2 tablespoons coarse sea salt

2–3 fresh sage leaves

1 boneless pork loin roast, about 1.5 kg/ 3 lb.

serves 4–6

Two days before serving, mix all the ingredients in a large ceramic or glass bowl. Cover and refrigerate for 2 days, turning the pork regularly.

When ready to cook, remove the pork from the marinade and put it in a roasting pan. Add the vegetables and flavourings from the marinade. Cook in a preheated oven at 200°C (400°F) Gas 6, basting occasionally with the marinade liquid, for 1½ hours. Serve immediately.

pork loin roasted with rosemary and garlic

Redolent of early morning Italian markets where porchetta (whole pigs roasted overnight in wood-fired ovens) is sold sliced and crammed into huge bread rolls as a morning snack, this dish recreates all those tastes and smells in your oven at home. Use as much rosemary as you can so the sweet pork flesh will be suffused with its pungent aroma.

1.8 kg/4 lb. loin of pork on the bone

4 large garlic cloves

4 tablespoons/¼ cup chopped fresh rosemary needles

a bunch of rosemary sprigs

extra virgin olive oil, for rubbing and sautéing

300 ml/scant 1¼ cups dry white wine

sea salt and freshly ground black pepper

serves 6

Ask the butcher to bone the loin, but to give you the bones. Also ask him to remove the skin and score it to make the crackling. Turn the loin fat side down. Make deep slits all over the meat, especially in the thick part. Make a paste of the garlic, chopped rosemary, at least 1 teaspoon of salt and pepper in a food processor. Push this paste into all the slits in the meat and spread the remainder over the surface of the meat. Roll up and tie with fine string, incorporating some long sprigs of rosemary along its length. Weigh the meat and calculate the cooking time, allowing 25 minutes for every 500 g/ 1 lb. At this stage you can wrap it and leave it in the refrigerator for several hours to deepen the flavour.

When ready to cook, heat 2 tablespoons olive oil in a frying pan/skillet, unwrap the pork and brown all over. Set in a roasting pan and pour the wine over the pork. Tuck in the remaining rosemary sprigs. Place the bones in another roasting pan convex side up. Rub the pork skin with a little oil and salt. Drape the skin over the pork bones. Place the pan of crackling on the top shelf of a preheated oven, and the pork on the bottom to middle shelf. Roast at 230°C (450°F) Gas 8 for 20 minutes then reduce the heat to 200°C (400°F) Gas 6, and roast for the remaining calculated time, basting the pork loin every 20 minutes.

When cooked, rest the pork in a warm place for 15 minutes before carving into thick slices. Serve with shards of crunchy crackling and the pan juices – there is no better gravy!

roast loin of pork with balsamic vinegar

This moist and tender cut of pork is basted throughout cooking with the mahogany-coloured balsamic vinegar and soy cooking juices that give a wonderful colour and flavour to the meat. Roasting first at a high temperature really crisps up the crackling and concentrates the sauce.

1.75 kg/4 lb. loin of pork

1 tablespoon olive oil

300 ml/1¼ cups dry white wine

75 ml/⅓ cup balsamic vinegar

75 ml/⅓ cup soy sauce

sea salt and freshly ground black pepper

serves 6

Ask the butcher to remove the rind and score it for crackling, then bone the loin and tie up the meat, but to give you the bones. Weigh the meat and calculate the cooking time, allowing 25 minutes to every 500 g/1 lb.

Heat the oil in a frying pan/skillet, add the meat, brown it all over, then transfer to a roasting pan and pour the wine, vinegar and soy sauce over the pork.

Put the bones in another roasting pan, convex side up. Rub the pork rind with salt, then drape it over the pork bones. Put the pan of crackling on the top shelf of the oven, and the meat on the bottom to middle shelf. Roast in a preheated oven at 220°C (425°F) Gas 7 for 30 minutes, baste the pork, then reduce the heat to 190°C (375°F) Gas 5, and roast for the remaining calculated time, basting the pork loin every 20 minutes. When cooked, serve the pork thickly sliced with shards of crunchy crackling and dark pan juices seasoned with freshly ground black pepper.

Reduced balsamic vinegar To make cheap balsamic vinegar taste rich and delicious, turn it into a concentrated syrup by pouring the whole bottle into a saucepan. Open the kitchen window or turn on the extractor/exhaust fan, then boil hard until reduced by half and looking syrupy. Let cool, then pour into a jar and store in the refrigerator. This is wonderful added to stews, soups and dressings.

shoulder of lamb with roasted vegetables

A shoulder of lamb is generally an affordable cut all year round, and slow-cooked in this way it's truly delicious and guaranteed to satisfy the hungriest of guests.

1.3–1.5 kg/3–3¼ lbs. shoulder of lamb, on the bone

500 ml/2 cups dry white wine

250 ml/1 cup freshly squeezed lemon juice

3 tablespoons olive oil

4 sprigs of fresh rosemary

2 teaspoons dried oregano, preferably Greek

4 garlic cloves, lightly smashed

1 large courgette/zucchini, roughly chopped

1 large red onion, cut into thin wedges

1 small yellow bell pepper, deseeded and thickly sliced

3 waxy potatoes, thickly sliced

1 tablespoon finely chopped dill

a handful of fresh flat leaf parsley leaves, roughly chopped

sea salt and freshly ground black pepper

serves 4

Put the lamb, skin-side up, in a non-metal dish. Add the wine, lemon juice, 2 tablespoons of the olive oil, the rosemary, oregano and garlic. Cover and refrigerate overnight.

Remove from the refrigerator 1 hour before cooking and season the skin of the lamb well with salt and pepper.

Preheat the oven to 220°C (425°F) Gas 7.

Remove the lamb from the marinade, reserving 2 tablespoons of the liquid. Roll it firmly and secure with kitchen string.

Put the courgette/zucchini, onion, yellow bell pepper and potatoes in a bowl with the reserved marinade and use your hands to toss the vegetables until well coated.

Set a roasting pan over high heat and add the remaining olive oil. Heat until very hot. Add the lamb and cook for 5–6 minutes, turning often, until golden all over. Add the vegetables to the tin and cook for 2–3 minutes, turning the vegetables often. Transfer to the preheated oven and cook for 40 minutes, turning the vegetables after 20 minutes. Transfer the vegetables to a bowl, cover with foil and keep warm until ready to serve.

Reduce the oven temperature to 180°C (350°F) Gas 4. Cook the lamb for a further hour, until the skin is dark and crisp. Remove from the oven and cover tightly with foil. Let rest in a warm place for 20 minutes before carving.

Add the dill and parsley to the warm vegetables and season to taste with salt and pepper.

To serve, plate thick slices of the lamb and serve the vegetables on the side.

Italian roast leg of lamb with lemon and anchovy sauce

There are so many flavours that can be introduced to the classic leg of lamb and each country has its favourites. Britain likes it just plain with mint sauce, Australians, New Zealanders and French stick it with slivers of garlic and sprigs of rosemary, while Italians love the combined flavour of lemon and garlic, with the salty seasoning in the gravy supplied by anchovies. Be adventurous – ask the butcher to tunnel-bone a more mature lamb and season the centre with crushed juniper berries.

1 leg of lamb, about 2.5–3 kg/6 lb.

2 garlic cloves, thinly sliced

1 tablespoon olive oil

175 ml/1¾ cups white wine

sea salt and freshly ground black pepper

sauce

5 anchovy fillets

175 ml/1¾ cups chicken stock

grated lemon zest from 1 unwaxed lemon

1 tablespoon chopped fresh flat leaf parsley

an instant-read thermometer

serves 5

Make slits in the meat in several places and insert the slivers of garlic. Brush the lamb with the oil and season with salt and pepper. Set it in a roasting pan and pour the wine around. Roast in a preheated oven at 200°C (400°F) Gas 6 until an instant-read thermometer registers 63°C (145°F) for medium rare or cook at 170°C (325°F) Gas 3 for well done meat until the thermometer registers 77°C (170°F). This takes 1¼–1½ hours. Baste the meat from time to time, adding water if the wine becomes low.

When the lamb is cooked to your liking, transfer it to a serving dish and let rest in a warm place while you make the gravy. Discard any excess fat from the roasting pan, then add the anchovies, crushing them to a paste with a fork. Stir in the stock until the anchovies have been absorbed. Add the lemon zest and parsley and any juices that have come out of the lamb during the resting period, then pour into a sauceboat to serve.

rack of lamb with cranberry sauce

This is the perfect way to cook lamb chops if you don't know exactly when you are going to have to dish them up, because they can wait for up to 2 hours before finishing them. To French-trim two 6-or 7-rib racks for 4 people, ask the butcher to cut away each backbone where it joins the ribs – this is called 'chining'. Now that the ribs are free, you can cut the racks in half between the middle ribs and discard the end rib on the half that has 4 (or keep them for a cook's treat later). Shorten the ribs to about 3–4 cm/1–1½ inches beyond the meat, then cut out the meat between each rib and scrape the bones clean. All these trimmings can be used to make stock.

2 racks of lamb, French-trimmed
(see recipe introduction)

about 500 g/4 cups baby spinach, wilted

marinating syrup

2 tablespoons cranberry sauce

125 ml/½ cup sweet sherry

125 ml/½ cup sherry vinegar

3 tablespoons sugar

2 tablespoons soy sauce

2 sprigs of rosemary

2 small garlic cloves, sliced

gravy

25 g/3–4 tablespoons unsalted butter

125 ml/½ cup white vermouth

250 ml/1 cup lamb or chicken stock

sea salt and freshly ground black pepper

serves 4–6

To make the marinating syrup, put the cranberry sauce in a saucepan, add the sherry, vinegar, sugar, soy sauce, rosemary and 3 slices of the garlic and boil to reduce and form a syrup. Brush the syrup all over the racks of lamb and put them in a plastic bag, with the rest of the syrup and set aside to marinate for 2 hours, turning them every 30 minutes.

When ready to cook, wipe the excess marinade off the racks of lamb, set them on non-stick parchment paper or a sheet of kitchen foil in a roasting pan and roast in a preheated oven at 250°C (500°F) Gas 9 for 8 minutes. Remove from the oven and let rest in a warm place for up to 2 hours.

To serve, reheat the racks for 6–8 minutes in the very hot oven, then slice them between the bones. Put a bed of cooked spinach on each plate, then put the cutlets on top, crossing over the bones.

Meanwhile, to make the gravy, put the butter in a small saucepan, add the vermouth and boil until reduced by half. Add the stock and 2–3 teaspoons of the marinade, bring to the boil and reduce again to improve the flavour. Season to taste with salt and pepper, pour around the meat, then serve.

pot roast leg of lamb with rosemary and onion gravy

The perfect cook-and-forget roast. The meat is cooked on a bed of rosemary and onions until it is completely tender all the way through – no pink bits – and the onions are melting into the rosemary gravy. Purée the meat juices with the soft onions for a wonderful, creamy sauce.

1.5 kg/3 lb. leg of lamb

2 tablespoons olive oil

3 garlic cloves, crushed

2 tablespoons chopped fresh rosemary

3 large rosemary sprigs

2 fresh bay leaves

4 large onions, thinly sliced

300 ml/1¼ cups dry white wine

2 teaspoons Dijon mustard

sea salt and freshly ground black pepper

serves 6

Trim the lamb of any excess fat. Heat the oil in a casserole in which the lamb will fit snugly. Add the lamb and brown it all over. Remove to a plate and let cool.

Crush the garlic and chopped rosemary together with a mortar and pestle. Using a small sharp knife, make little incisions all over the lamb. Push the paste well into these incisions. Season well with salt and pepper.

Put the rosemary sprigs, bay leaves and onions in the casserole dish and put the lamb on top. Mix the wine with the mustard, then pour into the casserole. Bring to the boil, cover tightly, then cook in a preheated oven at 160°C (325°F) Gas 3 for 1½ hours, turning the lamb over twice.

Raise the oven temperature to 200°C (400°F) Gas 6 and remove the lid from the casserole dish. Cook for another 30 minutes. The lamb should be very tender and completely cooked through.

Carefully remove the lamb to a serving dish and keep it warm. Skim the fat from the cooking juices and remove the bay leaves and rosemary sprigs. Add a little water if too thick, then bring to the boil, scraping the bottom of the pan to mix in the sediment. Pour the sauce into a blender or food processor and blend until smooth. Taste and season with salt and pepper. Serve with the lamb.

slow-roasted lamb shanks with chillies

The lower part of the lamb leg, with all the delicious melting gelatinous threads running through, is often a favourite cut. Shanks are much more tender than the equivalent shin of beef.

4 lamb shanks

2 tablespoons olive oil

tex-mex spices*

½ teaspoon garlic powder

½ teaspoon ground red chilli

½ teaspoon dried oregano

½ teaspoon hot chilli flakes

1 teaspoon salt

½ teaspoon coarsely ground black pepper

Roast Potatoes (page 170), to serve

sauce

1 tablespoon olive oil

2 garlic cloves, crushed

2 teaspoons hot oak-smoked paprika

1 teaspoon ground cumin

1 tablespoon red wine vinegar

6 beef or large tomatoes, skinned, halved and deseeded

2 tablespoons chopped fresh mint

½ teaspoon sugar

sea salt and freshly ground black pepper

red kidney beans

400 g/14 oz. cooked or canned red kidney beans

1 tablespoon olive oil

sea salt and freshly ground black pepper

serves 4

Brush the shanks with the olive oil. Put the garlic powder, ground red chilli, oregano, chilli flakes, salt and pepper in a bowl, mix well, then sprinkle over the shanks.

Set the shanks end to end in a roasting pan. Put in the middle of a preheated oven and cook at at 150°C (300°F) Gas 2 for 2 hours, turning them over 2–3 times. Remove from the oven and let rest for 30 minutes.

To make the sauce, heat the oil in a large pan, add the garlic and cook to a light brown (it will give off a delicious roasting aroma). Add the paprika and cumin and cook for 1 minute without letting them burn. Pour in the vinegar, then add the tomatoes, breaking them up with a wooden spoon and cooking to form a lumpy sauce. Add the mint, season with salt and pepper and add sugar to taste.

To prepare the red kidney beans, drain and transfer to a small saucepan, stir in the olive oil, add salt and pepper to taste, then heat gently.

Dish up the shanks, pour off any excess fat and add 2–3 tablespoons water to the tin to make a little stock. Stir well, then add it to the sauce. Bring to the boil, then season with salt and pepper and add more sugar if necessary. Pour the sauce over the meat and serve with roast potatoes and red kidney beans.

* Many supermarkets sell ready-made Tex-Mex spice mixes. Use 1½ tablespoons and mix with the salt.

shoulder of lamb with mountain herbs

Think of ravishingly pretty lavender fields in Provence, pungent basil, tarragon and rosemary scenting the air at weekend markets – wild, scrubby herb plants, stretching up into the Alpilles of Haute-Provence, and used to flavour all sorts of meat. Lamb and mutton taste splendid when teamed with these herbs: wild thyme, oregano, bay, savory, even wild juniper. A little wild garlic leaf, if available, might also be added.

1.75–2-kg/4–4½-lb. shoulder of lamb, ideally from a rare breed

4 garlic cloves, crushed

6 canned anchovy fillets

a small handful of fresh thyme leaves

a small handful of fresh oregano or marjoram leaves, chopped

a small handful of fresh mint leaves, chopped

100 g/1 cup fresh breadcrumbs

2 tablespoons Dijon mustard, plus extra to serve

4 tablespoons/¼ cup salted capers, rinsed and dried

salt and freshly ground black pepper

a handful of fresh wild garlic, sorrel, chard or borage greens

6 tablespoons red wine

a little stock or water

cornichons (tiny gherkins)

serves 6–8

Get your butcher to remove all tendons and tough connective tissue from the joint. Also ask him to slip a knife around and under the blade bone to create 2 neat pockets; this will nearly sever the joint, but keep it attached at one edge.

Put the garlic, anchovies, thyme, oregano and mint into a food processor and pulse, in short bursts, until roughly chopped. Add the breadcrumbs, mustard, capers and seasoning. Pulse repeatedly until roughly mixed.

Preheat the oven to 220°C (425°F) Gas 7.

Push the garlic greens up inside the two pockets, one above and one below the bone, and add half the breadcrumb stuffing to each one. Secure the two edges of the meat by skewering with satay skewers. Criss-cross the string around these to keep everything in place, and fasten with a knot.

Place the lamb in a large roasting pan and pour in the wine. Roast for 30 minutes, then reduce the heat to 180°C (350°F) Gas 4, and cook for 50–55 minutes more. (As a guide, allow 15 minutes per 450 g/pound after the initial 30-minute hot-roasting.)

Remove the satay skewers and string from the cooked lamb, and let the roast stand in a warm place for 5–8 minutes.

Add a little boiling water or stock to the pan juices, if necessary, stir well, then pour into a sauce boat. Offer cornichons and Dijon mustard as accompaniments.

Indian spiced leg of lamb cooked in a salt crust, with raita

This is a simple way to cook lamb – coat it in a thick crust and roast it in the oven. The aromas from the spices are intoxicating, especially the fresh curry leaves hidden in the crust.

1.3 kg/3 lb. leg of lamb, bone in

4 garlic cloves, sliced

spice rub

20 green cardamom pods, bashed

1 teaspoon cumin seeds

1 cinnamon stick, broken into pieces

½ teaspoon whole cloves

½ teaspoon turmeric

½ teaspoon chipotle chilli powder

½ teaspoon Spanish smoked paprika

2 tablespoons olive oil

salt crust

550 g/2½ cups coarse sea salt

450 g/3½ cups plain/all-purpose flour

1 small bunch fresh curry leaves

raita

225 ml/1 cup natural/plain yogurt

2 garlic cloves, finely chopped

1 small cucumber, grated

2 tablespoons fresh mint leaves, torn

sea salt

ground sumac, to sprinkle

serves 6–8

Wash the leg of lamb and pat dry. Using a sharp knife, stab the lamb all over and stud with the slices of garlic. Set the lamb aside.

Put all the dry ingredients for the Spice Rub in a saucepan and dry roast over low heat, stirring continuously until they are lightly toasted. Pound the toasted spices to a rough mixture using a pestle and mortar. Add the olive oil and stir to a paste. Spread the paste all over the lamb and chill in the refrigerator for at least 2 hours or for up to 24 hours.

When ready to cook the lamb, preheat the oven to 200°C (400°F) Gas 6.

To make the Salt Crust, mix the salt, flour and curry leaves together in a bowl with 250 ml/1 cup water to give a doughy consistency. If the mixture is too dry, add more water 1 tablespoon at a time. Roll out on a floured worktop to twice the size of the lamb. Put the lamb leg at one end of the pastry and fold over the remaining dough. Seal, making sure there are no holes for any steam to escape. Put in a lightly oiled roasting tin and bake in the preheated oven for 1 hour.

Take the lamb out of the oven and leave to rest for 10–15 minutes.

To make the Raita, mix together the yogurt, garlic, grated cucumber and mint leaves. Season with sea salt and sprinkle with the sumac. Refrigerate until needed.

To serve the lamb, peel off the crust and place on a wooden board to carve. Serve with the Raita.

honey-roasted spiced lamb

Traditionally, this is a festive Moroccan dish, as an entire lamb or kid is roasted slowly over embers over a pit dug in the ground and shared among a community or a large family. When cooking a joint of lamb in a communal oven, Moroccan cooks often add seasonal fruit, such as fresh figs, plums, apricots or quince to the dish – this is a delightful option for you too.

a leg of lamb, about 2 kg/5 lb.

200 ml/¾ cup water

2–3 tablespoons honey

10–12 pieces of fresh fruit, such as figs, plums or apricots (optional)

a bunch of fresh coriander/cilantro leaves, roughly chopped

sea salt and freshly ground black pepper

for the coating

4 garlic cloves, chopped

40 g/a 2½-inch piece of fresh ginger, peeled and chopped

1 red chilli, deseeded and chopped

a generous pinch of sea salt

a small bunch each of fresh coriander/cilantro and flat leaf parsley, chopped

1–2 teaspoons ground cumin

1–2 teaspoons ground coriander

3 tablespoons softened butter or olive oil

serves 6

First, make the coating. Using a mortar and pestle, pound the garlic, ginger and chilli with enough salt to form a coarse paste. Add the fresh coriander/cilantro and parsley, pound to a paste and stir in the ground cumin and coriander. Put the butter or olive oil in a bowl and beat in the paste until thoroughly mixed. Cut small incisions in the leg of lamb with a sharp knife and rub the spicy coating all over the meat, making sure it goes into the incisions. Cover and leave in the refrigerator for at least 2 hours.

Preheat the oven to 200°C (400°F) Gas 4. Transfer the leg of lamb to a roasting dish and pour the water around it. Roast in the preheated oven for about 1 hour 15 minutes, basting from time to time, until it is nicely browned. Spoon the honey over the lamb and place the fresh figs, plums or apricots around the meat, if using. Return the dish to the oven for a further 15 minutes.

Put the roasted lamb in a serving dish and leave it to rest for about 15 minutes before serving. Meanwhile, heat the juices in the roasting dish, season with salt and pepper, and pour over the roast lamb. Sprinkle the coriander/cilantro over the top and, if using fruit, arrange it around the dish.

butterflied leg of lamb with mediterranean stuffing

Your butcher will butterfly the joint for you, but if you want to do it yourself, hold a very sharp knife like a dagger and cut from the fleshy end of the leg to the opposite end. Then let your knife follow the bones, cutting the flesh away so that the meat opens out like a butterfly.

1.5-kg/3½-lb. leg of lamb, butterflied

stuffing

leaves from 2 sprigs of rosemary

2 red onions, finely chopped

3 garlic cloves, finely chopped

75 g/½ cup olives, pitted and chopped

1 courgette/zucchini, grated and squeezed dry

1 egg

1 tablespoon olive oil

sea salt and freshly ground black pepper

gravy

2 tablespoons plain/all-purpose flour

1 teaspoon tomato purée/paste

3 tablespoons redcurrant jelly

100 ml/⅓ cup red wine

200 ml/1 cup vegetable stock

sea salt and freshly ground black pepper

serves 6

Preheat the oven to 190°C (375°F) Gas 5, then lightly oil a roasting pan.

Combine all the stuffing ingredients and season. Open out the leg of lamb, skin-side down, and spread the stuffing over it. Fold the lamb back together and tie securely with string. Place the lamb in the prepared pan and roast for 1 hour and 20 minutes. When cooked, transfer the lamb to a carving plate and keep warm.

Pour half the fat out of the roasting pan, add the flour and mix until smooth. Stir in the tomato purée/paste and redcurrant jelly, then pour in the wine and stock, mixing thoroughly. Place the pan directly on the heat and stir constantly until the gravy thickens. Adjust the seasoning and press the gravy through a sieve/strainer to remove any lumps. Cut the string from the lamb and carve. Serve with mashed potatoes and green beans.

poultry

roast chicken with lemon, thyme and potato stuffing

Roast chicken is the perfect meal to enjoy on a Sunday at home with the family. It's always worth cooking a larger bird than you need because the leftovers can be used in a pilaf or to make sandwiches. You can also use the carcass to make stock and freeze it for making soup or risotto. Three meals for the price of one bird!

1 medium free-range chicken

1 unwaxed lemon, thinly sliced

4 bay leaves

4 bacon slices

stuffing

2 garlic cloves, crushed

1 onion, finely diced

leaves from 4 sprigs of thyme

1 large potato, coarsely grated

300 g/10½ oz. sausagemeat

zest and juice of 1 unwaxed lemon

sea salt and freshly ground black pepper

gravy

25 g/2 tablespoons plain/all-purpose flour

500 ml/2 cups chicken stock

sea salt and freshly ground black pepper

serves 4

Preheat the oven to 180°C (350°F) Gas 4. Lightly oil a roasting pan.

Take the chicken and carefully slide your hand between the skin and the breast meat. Insert the lemon slices under the skin along with the bay leaves.

To make the stuffing, put the garlic, onion, thyme, potato and sausagemeat in a large bowl. Add the lemon zest and juice, season and mix well to combine. Cut any excess fat from the cavity of the chicken, then stuff the bird with the potato mixture.

Weigh your chicken to work out the cooking time: you should allow 20 minutes per 500 g/1 lb. 2 oz., plus 20 minutes extra. Put the chicken in the prepared roasting pan and lay the bacon slices over the breast. Put in the hot oven and cook for the time you have calculated. When the chicken is ready, remove it from the roasting pan and keep warm.

Now make the gravy. Add the flour to the pan and stir with a wooden spoon to combine with the fat and juices. Slowly pour in the chicken stock, stirring continuously to prevent lumps forming. Place the roasting pan directly on the heat and bring to the boil. When the mixture has thickened, remove it from the heat and season well. If you like a very smooth gravy, press it through a sieve/strainer with the back of a spoon.

Carve the chicken and serve with plenty of the stuffing and the hot gravy.

brined roast chicken with a ham and fresh sage stuffing

Brining is the most basic of marinades. Prepared and cooked this way, your roast chicken will be full of flavour and truly memorable. If you are pressed for time, you can leave out the brining, but it adds a delicious depth of flavour if you do. If you are brining, do bear in mind that the chicken will need to be in the liquid for at least three hours and removed from the brine one hour before cooking.

3 tablespoons sea salt

2 tablespoons granulated white sugar

2 fresh or dried bay leaves

1 chicken, about 1.8 kg/4 lb.

2 tablespoons butter, softened

ham and fresh sage stuffing

5 slices of stale white bread, crusts removed, roughly torn

2 tablespoons butter

1 small onion, finely chopped

2 garlic cloves, chopped

100 g/3½ oz. smoked ham, finely chopped

2 tablespoons finely chopped fresh sage

1 egg

serves 4

Put the salt, sugar and bay leaves in a very large saucepan with 3 litres/12 cups water. Bring to the boil, stirring a few times until the salt and sugar have dissolved, then remove from the heat. Let cool to room temperature. Put the chicken in the non-reactive bowl and pour in the liquid so that the chicken is fully immersed. Cover and put somewhere cold to sit for 3–6 hours.

To make the stuffing, put the bread in a food processor and process to make coarse crumbs. Tip the crumbs into a bowl and set aside.

Heat the butter in a saucepan set over medium heat and cook the onion for 5 minutes, until softened. Add the garlic, ham and sage and stir-fry for 1 minute. Add the mixture to the crumbs with the egg and use your hands to combine well.

Remove the chicken from the brine 1 hour before cooking and keep refrigerated.

Preheat the oven to 170°C (325°F) Gas 3.

Spoon the stuffing into the cavity of the chicken and tie the legs firmly together with kitchen string.

Put the chicken in a roasting pan and rub the butter over the top side. Roast in the preheated oven for 1½ hours, until the skin of the chicken is golden and the meat is cooked through. Let the chicken rest in a warm place for 15 minutes before carving. Carve the chiken and serve with plenty of the stuffing on the side.

Sonoran spiced orange chicken

This makes a moist, spicy dish for a light lunch. If you would like a more fiery taste, increase the quantity of dried chilli/hot pepper flakes and use hot paprika. This dish would also be delicious served with tacos for a picnic. Just reduce the gravy juices to make a concentrated sauce and serve with plenty of crunchy green salad.

1 chicken, about 1.5 kg/3 lb. 5 oz.

1 tablespoon olive oil

2 teaspoons sweet oak-smoked paprika

½ teaspoon crushed dried chilli/hot pepper flakes

2 teaspoons ground cumin

1 teaspoon ground cinnamon

1 tablespoon chopped fresh oregano or marjoram

1 unwaxed orange

1–2 tablespoons unsalted butter

sea salt and freshly ground black pepper

an instant-read thermometer

serves 4

Loosen the skin around the cavity of the bird and ease the skin away from the breast. Pour in ½ tablespoon of the oil and massage it around underneath the skin with your fingertips.

Put the paprika, dried chilli/hot pepper flakes, cumin, cinnamon and 1 teaspoon of the chopped oregano in a bowl, stir well, then push half the mixture under the skin of the chicken.

Cut 2 slices off the top of the orange and cut the rest in quarters. Push the slices under the skin on each side of the breast. Rub the outside of the bird with the remaining oil and spices. Put the butter, the remaining herbs, the orange quarters, salt, pepper and 2 tablespoons water in the cavity.

Put the bird in a roasting pan and roast in the middle of a preheated oven at 170°C (325°F) Gas 3 for 1½ hours, basting from time to time, until an instant-read thermometer registers 82°C (180°F) at the thickest part of the leg.

To serve, remove the bird from the oven and pour the juices out of the cavity into the pan – squeeze the juice from the orange quarters and discard the skins. Stir the juices and spoon them over the chicken when it is served.

Carve the chicken and serve with the delicious roasting juices sponed over the top.

quick-roasted chicken pieces with tomatoes, mushrooms and brandy on crusty croutes

This delicious recipe can be so easily varied with other ingredients – try marinating the chicken in some curry paste or just add olives and gherkins to the sauce. Serve it with spinach or any other green vegetable. Croutes of fried bread are a traditional French accompaniment and are perfect for soaking up the tasty sauce.

4 large chicken pieces, such as breasts or whole legs

1 teaspoon olive oil

sauce

100 g/3½ oz. unsalted butter

1 teaspoon fresh thyme leaves

2 bay leaves

4 shallots

2 beef tomatoes, skinned and deseeded

250 g/9 oz. portobello mushrooms, sliced

100 ml/½ cup brandy

sea salt and freshly ground black pepper

crusty croutes (optional)

4 slices white bread, crusts removed

3 tablespoons unsalted butter, or melted clarified butter

serves 4

Put the chicken pieces skin side down in a roasting pan, brush them with the oil and roast in a preheated oven at 220°C (425°F) Gas 7 for 10 minutes.

Meanwhile, to make the sauce, heat the butter in a frying pan/skillet, add the thyme, bay leaves and shallots and sauté until softened but not browned. Add the tomatoes and mushrooms and simmer until the liquid disappears and the tomato mixture starts to brown. Add the brandy, salt and pepper.

Remove the pan from the oven, turn the chicken pieces over, spoon the sauce around, then reduce the heat to 160°C (325°F) Gas 3 and return to the oven for a further 30 minutes.

Serve each piece of chicken on a square of crisp fried bread* with plenty of sauce spooned over the top.

* To make the crusty croutes, spread the slices of bread generously with the butter and set on a metal tray in a preheated oven at 230°C (450°F) Gas 8 for 10 minutes or until golden brown. Turn once during cooking. Alternatively, you can dip them in melted clarified butter and fry on both sides in a hot pan until crisp. Drain on paper towels.

roast chicken stuffed with couscous, apricots and dates

This Moroccan-style roast chicken with its hearty and succulent stuffing is perfect for entertaining friends and family. Stuffed with aromatic, fruity couscous, this dish is really a meal on its own, accompanied by a fresh, green salad.

2 garlic cloves, crushed

2 teaspoons dried oregano or thyme

1–2 teaspoons paprika

2 tablespoons butter, softened

1 large chicken, about 1.5 kg/3 lb. 5 oz.

1 sliced off orange end

150 ml/⅔ cup chicken stock

for the couscous stuffing

225 g/1½ cups couscous

½ teaspoon salt

225 ml/scant 1 cup warm water

1 tablespoon olive oil

1–2 teaspoons ground cinnamon

1 teaspoon ground coriander

½ teaspoon ground cumin

1 tablespoon clear honey

2 tablespoons golden raisins

125 g/½ cup ready-to-eat dried apricots, thickly sliced

125 g/½ cup ready-to-eat dates, thickly sliced or chopped

2–3 tablespoons blanched almonds, roasted

a green salad, to serve

serves 4–6

Preheat the oven to 180°C (350°F) Gas 4. To make the stuffing, tip the couscous into a large bowl. Stir the salt into the warm water and pour it over the couscous, stirring all the time so that the water is absorbed evenly. Leave the couscous to swell for about 10 minutes then, using your fingers, rub the oil into the couscous to break up the lumps and aerate it. Stir in the other stuffing ingredients and set aside.

In a small bowl, beat the garlic, oregano and paprika into the softened butter then smear it all over the chicken, inside and out. Put the chicken in the base of a tagine or in an ovenproof dish and fill the cavity with as much of the couscous stuffing as you can (any left-over couscous can be heated through in the oven before serving and fluffed up with a little extra oil or butter). Seal the cavity with the slice of orange (you can squeeze the juice from the rest of the orange over the chicken). Pour the stock into the base of the tagine and roast the chicken in the oven for 1–1½ hours, basting from time to time, until the chicken is cooked.

Remove the chicken from the oven and allow it to rest for 10 minutes before carving or jointing it and strain the cooking juices into a jug/pitcher. Heat up any remaining couscous (as described above) and serve this with the chicken, plenty of the cooking juices to pour over the top and a green salad on the side.

roasted spring chicken with herbs and ricotta

Buying your chicken at a farmers' market is the very best way to guarantee the meat is of the highest quality. Many stalls will provide brochures or have a website showing where the animal has come from so that you can be sure it had a good home before it made it into your kitchen. Rubbing the herb and ricotta mixture between the skin and meat of the chicken keeps the flesh moist and ensures the whole bird stays succulent. It may seem over indulgent to roast a chicken with cheese but ricotta is surprisingly low in fat and tastes delicious with the fresh herbs in this recipe.

250 g/1 cup ricotta cheese

2 tablespoons finely chopped fresh basil

3 tablespoons finely chopped flat leaf parsley leaves

2 garlic cloves, chopped

2 tablespoons light olive oil

1 teaspoon sea salt

grated zest and freshly squeezed juice of 1 unwaxed lemon

1 chicken, weighing about 1 kg/ 2 lb. 4 oz.

2 lemons, cut in half

serves 2

Preheat the oven to 180ºC (350ºF) Gas 4.

Put the ricotta in a bowl with the basil, parsley, garlic, 1 tablespoon of the olive oil, sea salt, lemon juice and zest and mix well.

Wash and dry the chicken with paper towels. Use your hands to carefully separate the skin from the meat, without tearing the skin, and force the ricotta mixture between the skin and the meat. Rub the extra cut lemon halves over the chicken then place them in the cavity of the bird. Tie the legs together with some kitchen string. Transfer the chicken to a plate, cover with clingfilm/plastic wrap and set aside for 30 minutes.

Put a roasting pan in the preheated oven for 10 minutes to heat up. Pour the remaining olive oil into the roasting pan. Sprinkle sea salt over the chicken, then put the chicken in the pan and roast in the preheated oven for 1 hour.

Remove the chicken from the oven, cover with aluminium foil and let cool for 15 minutes before carving. Carve the chicken and serve with the delicious juices from the roasting pan.

chicken with forty cloves of garlic

This classic dish from Provence uses all the best-loved flavours of the region such as fresh herbs, olive oil and of course a large amount of garlic. The long cooking makes the garlic meltingly tender and sweet. Serve the chicken with the garlic, which can be squeezed out of the skins and spread onto crisp toasts.

1 chicken weighing about 2 kg/4 lb. 8 oz.

2 lemons, sliced

4 sprigs of thyme

a few large sprigs of rosemary

a few sprigs of sage

5 bay leaves

200 ml/¾ cup olive oil

40 unpeeled fat garlic cloves

500 g/4 cups plain/all-purpose flour

sea salt and freshly ground black pepper

12 thin croûtes or toasts, to serve

serves 4

Season the cavity of the bird with salt and pepper. Add the sliced lemon and 2 sprigs of thyme. Push 2 sprigs of thyme, 2 sprigs of rosemary, 2 sprigs of sage and 2 bay leaves between the skin and the breast on both sides of the chicken. Pour the olive oil into a casserole dish and turn the chicken around in it to coat it all over. Add the garlic cloves and remaining herbs and mix with the oil to coat. Sprinkle with salt and pepper.

Mix the flour with enough water to make into a soft dough. Roll the dough into a long cylinder and press it around the edge of the casserole dish. Push the lid down on top and press any overhanging dough up and over the edge of the lid to seal.

Bake in a preheated oven at 180°C (350°F) Gas 4 for 1½ hours. By this time, the chicken will be cooked, but will happily sit unopened for 15–20 minutes. Take the dish to the table, crack open the crust and lift off the lid to release the aroma of Provence.

Carve or joint the chicken and serve each portion with the cooking juices and a pile of the sweet roasted garlic to spread on toasts.

jasmine-brined roasted poussins with salsa verde

Brining the poussins ensures a crispy skin when roasted. You can use any tea to make the brine, but jasmine tea infuses a floral taste into the poussins and creates a subtle flavour when cooked. Serve with the dark green salsa verde. You can also make this with Cornish game hen.

2 poussins weighing 700 g/1 lb. 9 oz. (or 1 Cornish game hen)

1 small unwaxed lemon

1 garlic clove, crushed

1 tablespoon olive oil

sea salt and freshly ground black pepper

brining solution

4 tablespoons jasmine tea or 4 jasmine teabags

1.5 litres/6 cups boiling water

60 g/½ cup coarse rock salt

1 tablespoon dark brown sugar

salsa verde

20 g/1 cup flat leaf parsley leaves

20 g/1 cup coriander/cilantro leaves

20 g/1 cup mint leaves

2 garlic cloves, finely chopped

finely grated zest of 1 small unwaxed lemon (see method)

1 tablespoon brined capers

125 ml/½ cup olive oil

serves 2

First make the brine. Put the jasmine tea in a large measuring jug/pitcher and pour over the boiling water. Add the salt and sugar and stir until dissolved. Set aside and leave to cool completely.

Wash and dry the poussins and put them in a deep dish. Pour the cooled brine over them, cover and refrigerate for 6–8 hours.

When you are ready to cook, preheat the oven to 190°C (375°F) Gas 5. Remove the poussins from the brining mixture and pat dry, removing any leftover tea leaves. Discard the brining mixture; it cannot be used again.

Place the poussins in a roasting pan. Zest the lemon and reserve for the Salsa Verde. Cut the lemon into quarters and stuff the cavity with them. Tie the legs together with kitchen string. Mix together the garlic and oil and rub over the skin of the poussins. Season with sea salt and freshly ground black pepper.

Roast in the preheated oven for 35 minutes until cooked and the poussin juices run clear.

To make the Salsa Verde, put all the salsa ingredients in a food processor and pulse until roughly chopped. Be careful not to overprocess; you want the salsa to be slightly chunky. Season with sea salt and black pepper.

When the poussins are ready, remove from the oven and set aside to rest for 10 minutes, covered with aluminium foil, in a warm place. Carve the poussins and serve with the Salsa Verde.

spatchcocked poussins with rosemary and lemon glaze

These little birds are easy to serve at a dinner when there is not much time for cooking. They take just over thirty minutes in the oven, and the juices make a delicious and simple gravy. Serve with potatoes and a simple fresh salad.

4–6 poussins

1 tablespoon freshly squeezed lemon juice

250 ml/1 cup chicken stock (optional)

1 tablespoon unsalted butter

1 tablespoon chopped fresh flat leaf parsley

sea salt and freshly ground black pepper

marinade

30 g/2 tablespoons unsalted butter

2 tablespoons extra virgin olive oil

2 teaspoons freshly grated lemon zest

a sprig of rosemary

2 garlic cloves, sliced

75 ml/scant ⅓ cup white wine

serves 4–6

To prepare the marinade, put the butter, olive oil, lemon zest, rosemary, garlic and wine in a saucepan and bring to the boil. Remove from the heat and let cool.

Put each bird breast side down on a work surface. Using kitchen scissors, cut along either side of the backbones and remove them.

Put the bones in a large saucepan, cover with cold water, bring to the boil and simmer for 30 minutes. Lift out the bones with tongs and boil down the stock to about 250 ml/1 cup. Set aside.*

Meanwhile, turn the birds breast side up and flatten the breastbones until you hear them crack. Flatten the birds further, folding the legs inward. Set them side-by-side in a roasting pan and sprinkle with salt and pepper. Pour over the marinade and transfer the pan to the refrigerator until 30 minutes or so before you start to cook.

Roast in the middle of a preheated oven at 240°C (475°F) Gas 8 for 35 minutes. Baste the birds with the juices after 20 minutes. When they are cooked, lift them onto a serving dish, stir the lemon juice into the pan juices, then stir in the stock, butter and parsley. Taste and adjust the seasoning with salt and pepper, then serve with the sauce spooned over the top.

* To save time, you can use store-bought chicken stock instead of making your own here.

roast turkey breast with olive salsa verde

Lean turkey meat pairs very well with strong flavours, so it works perfectly here with a sharp and tangy salsa. While it is usually a good idea to do plenty of preparation ahead of time when entertaining, here the salsa is definitely best made as close to the time that you intend to eat it as possible. It will oxidize very quickly and lose much of its vibrant fresh taste.

1 turkey breast, about 1.8 kg/4 lb., skin-on

2 tablespoons light olive oil

2 teaspoons smoked paprika (pimentón)

8 slices of prosciutto

sea salt and freshly ground black pepper

olive salsa verde

100 g/⅔ cup pitted green olives

3 baby gherkins (cornichons)

a bunch of fresh flat leaf parsley leaves

a large handful of fresh mint leaves

2 garlic cloves, chopped

3 anchovy fillets in olive oil, drained

3 tablespoons freshly squeezed lemon juice

125 ml/½ cup olive oil

to serve

Roast Potatoes (page 170)

Glazed Roast Carrots (page 178)

serves 6–8

Preheat the oven to 180ºC (350ºF) Gas 4.

Wash the turkey and pat it dry. Season the skin well with salt and pepper. Heat the light olive oil in a roasting pan set over high heat and cook the turkey, skin-side down, for 5 minutes, until the skin is golden. Remove the turkey from the pan, leaving any residual oil in the pan. Sprinkle the paprika over the skin. Lay the prosciutto slices side by side and slightly overlapping over the entire skin side of the turkey, tucking them in underneath the breast.

Return the turkey to the roasting pan, sitting it skin-side up. Cook in the preheated oven for 1¼ hours, basting occasionally with the pan juices. Increase the heat to 220°C (425°F) Gas 7 and cook for a further 10–15 minutes so that the prosciutto and skin is very crisp. Remove, and lightly cover in kitchen foil.

To make the olive salsa verde, put all of the ingredients in a food processor and process until well combined and coarsely chopped, but do not overprocess.

Carve the turkey and serve with the olive salsa verde over the top. Serve with roast potates and glazed roast carrots, if liked.

roast turkey with lemon and herb stuffing

Family tradition will dictate the best way to present a festive turkey but do try this recipe with two stuffings – one with fresh chestnuts for the neck cavity and the other a light herb and lemon bread stuffing made with plenty of butter, for the body cavity. Give yourself a generous 40 minutes at the end for the turkey to rest before serving.

1 turkey, with giblets

1 onion, coarsely chopped

a sprig of thyme

1 bay leaf

125 g/1 stick salted butter

sea salt and freshly ground black pepper

Lemon and Herb Stuffing (page 225)

Chestnut Stuffing (page 222)

to serve

Bacon Rolls (page 233)

Chipolatas (page 233)

Sausage Meat Patties (page 233)

Bread Sauce (page 229)

lightly boiled Brussels sprouts

Roast Potatoes (page 170)

for sizes, serving quantities and cooking times, see the chart on page 21

To make a stock, the day before, put the giblets, minus the liver, but with the neck chopped in half, in a saucepan. Add the onion, thyme and bay leaf. Cover with water and bring slowly to the boil, removing any foam as it rises. Simmer for 2 hours and strain. Taste and, if necessary, reduce to strengthen the flavour.

Wipe out the neck area and cavity of the turkey with a damp cloth and lightly season the inside. Spoon in the chosen stuffings, allowing space for each one to expand.

Put half the butter in a saucepan and melt gently. Spread the remaining butter all over the skin. Soak the muslin or paper in the melted butter and drape over the bird, with a double layer covering the drumsticks.

Preheat the oven to 180°C (350°F) Gas 4. Put the bird in a large roasting pan in the middle of the oven. Roast for the calculated time according to size (page 21) except that the oven temperature must be raised to 230°C (450°F) Gas 8 and the coverings removed for the last 30 minutes to crisp the skin. When the turkey is cooked, leave to rest for at least 40 minutes before serving.

Using oven mitts, or rubber gloves specially reserved for the occasion, tip out any free juices from the cavity, then lift the turkey onto the serving platter. Return it to the oven, leaving the door open until the temperature has dropped and will no longer cook the bird. Pour off the gravy juices into a jug/pitcher. Reheat with the seasoned stock. Use to fill a gravy boat, reserving the rest for second helpings. Serve with bacon rolls, chipolatas, sausage meat patties, bread sauce, brussels sprouts and roast potatoes.

rolled turkey breast with spinach, bacon and cheese

Stuffed turkey meat is often dry. If you add a juicy filling and buttery herb gravy, it will be transformed into a deliciously moist, light, lunch dish. Serve with baby new potatoes and Glazed Roast Carrots (page 178) for special occasions.

a small boneless breast of turkey, about 550 g/1 lb. 4 oz.

250 g/1¼ cups cooked chopped spinach

freshly grated nutmeg

4 slices of back bacon

250 g/9 oz. Cheddar or Gruyère cheese, thinly sliced

2 tablespoons olive or sunflower/safflower oil

sea salt and freshly ground black pepper

herb gravy

300 ml/1¼ cups strong chicken stock

175 g/1 stick unsalted butter

1 tablespoon chopped fresh flat leaf parsley

2 teaspoons chopped fresh tarragon

an instant-read thermometer

serves 4

Put the turkey breast skin side down on a flat board and hit it 2–3 times with the side of a heavy cleaver or meat mallet to flatten it. Cut a horizontal slice off the thickest part of the breast to even it up more, and use it to cover a thinner part. Season the turkey with salt and pepper and season the spinach with plenty of nutmeg.

Overlap the bacon slices to cover the inside surface of the meat and cover this with the spinach. Make a third layer with slices of cheese. Roll up the turkey into a roll and tie it neatly with kitchen string. Brush it all over with the oil. Roast in the middle of a preheated oven at 200°C (400°F) Gas 6 for 1 hour or until an instant-read thermometer measures 82°C (180°F). Baste the turkey frequently with some of the stock for the herb gravy.

When the turkey is done, remove from the oven and transfer to a serving dish. Remove and discard the string. Reserve any roasting juices and any more that collect in the serving dish.

To make the gravy, put the butter, remaining stock, parsley and tarragon in a saucepan and bring to the boil. Add the juices from the roasting pan and the serving dish.

Slice the turkey crossways and serve with the herb gravy.

roast ducklings with orange and ginger pilaf

While many of us love duck, most of us would admit to being a little bit afraid of cooking it at home. But fear not, you can't go wrong with this recipe! The ducklings are initially slow-cooked, rendering out much of the fat, and then blasted in a hot oven for the remainder of the cooking time, which produces a lovely, crisp skin.

2 ducklings, about 1.5–1.6 kg/ 3 lb. 5 oz.–3 lb. 8 oz. each

2 oranges

10-cm/4-inch piece of fresh ginger

2 tablespoons olive oil

1 tablespoon butter

6 shallots, thinly sliced

2 fresh or dried bay leaves

2 garlic cloves, chopped

400 g/scant 2 cups basmati rice

500 ml/2 cups chicken stock

a generous pinch of saffron threads

sea salt

watercress salad, to serve

serves 4

Preheat the oven to 130°C (250°F) Gas ½.

Trim the fatty area around the tail end of the ducklings. Tuck the neck and wings underneath the bird. Using a skewer, pierce the skin all over without piercing the flesh.

Grate the zest of one of the oranges and set aside. Cut both oranges in half. Squeeze both oranges to give 125 ml/½ cup juice. Put 2 of the halves in the cavity of each duckling. Thinly slice half of the ginger and put it in with the oranges. Grate the remaining ginger and set aside.

Rub the ducklings all over with salt. Sit them on a cooking rack set over a deep roasting pan. Cook in the preheated oven for 2 hours, basting every 30 minutes. Increase the oven temperature to 220°C (425°F) Gas 7 and pour 250 ml/1 cup water into the roasting pan. Return the ducklings to the oven and cook for a further 20–30 minutes, until the skin is golden and crisp. Remove from the oven and let rest for 30 minutes before carving.

Meanwhile, to make the pilaf, heat the oil and butter in a large heavy-based saucepan set over medium heat. Add the orange zest, grated ginger, shallots, bay leaves and garlic and cook, stirring, for 2–3 minutes, until softened. Add the rice and cook for 2 minutes, stirring to combine. Add the stock, orange juice and saffron. Stir a few times to remove any bits from the bottom of the pan and bring to the boil. Cover and cook over low heat for 20 minutes. Remove from the heat and stir. Set the cooked rice aside.

Serve the duckling with the pilaf on the side and a watercress salad, if liked.

roast duck with citrus fruits

Duck has a wonderful flavour, but it is a fatty meat, so this recipe contains citrus fruit to help cut through the richness. Do not be alarmed at the size of the duck specified; it loses a huge amount of fat during cooking, and has much less meat than a chicken of the same size.

1 3-kg/6 lb. 8 oz. duck
1 unwaxed lemon, thinly sliced
1 unwaxed orange, thinly sliced
1 unwaxed lime, thinly sliced

orange sauce
1 tablespoon plain/all-purpose flour
150 ml/⅔ cup vegetable stock
150 ml/⅔ cup orange juice
sea salt and freshly ground black pepper

to serve
Glazed Roast Carrots (page 181)
Roast Potatoes (page 170)

serves 4

Preheat the oven to 190ºC (375ºF) Gas 5. Lightly grease a roasting pan.

Put all the slices of citrus fruit in the cavity of the duck. Rub seasoning all over the skin. Place the duck on a roasting rack in the prepared pan; this is important so that the fat can drip out and the duck will not be sitting in it. Place in the oven and roast for 2½ hours.

When cooked, lift up the duck and pour the juices from the cavity into a heatproof jug/pitcher. Transfer the duck to a plate and keep warm while making the sauce.

To make the orange sauce, drain all but 1 tablespoon of fat from the roasting pan (save the excess in the fridge for general cooking purposes). Add the flour to the pan and mix thoroughly. Stir in the stock and orange juice, and add the reserved duck juices. Place over the heat and bring to the boil, stirring constantly. If you want a very smooth sauce, press the mixture through a sieve/strainer. Carve the duck and serve with glazed roast carrots, roast potatoes and the orange sauce.

roast duck à l'Alsacienne with sauerkraut and frankfurters

Duck is a rich meat and sauerkraut makes a perfect complement, both in flavour and goodness. Served with frankfurters and gammon, this becomes one of the traditional dishes of Alsace. It can be served with roast potatoes.

1 jar sauerkraut, about 800 g/1 lb. 12 oz.

250 g/9 oz. streaky bacon or smoked pork hock, cut into chunks or slices

12 frankfurters

1 duck, about 3 kg/6 lb. 8 oz.

sea salt and freshly ground black pepper

an instant-read thermometer

serves 6

Empty the sauerkraut into a saucepan. Cover with boiling water and bring to the boil again. Drain, discarding the water (unless you like very strong sauerkraut) and top up again with more water, then bring to the boil. Add the pieces of bacon or hock and simmer for 80 minutes. When the sauerkraut is tender, drain off this water into another saucepan, add the frankfurters and reheat just before serving (they are already cooked). Put the sauerkraut aside.

Meanwhile, sprinkle the duck with salt and pepper and put in a roasting pan without any oil. Roast in a preheated oven at 200°C (400°F) Gas 6 for 1½ hours, first on one side for 30 minutes, then the other for 20 minutes and finally on its back, or until an instant-read thermometer registers 82°C (180°F) at the thickest part of the thigh.

Remove the duck from the oven and let rest for 10 minutes. Remove the bird from the roasting pan, draining any juices from the cavity back into the pan. Put the duck on a carving board, pull back the legs and cut off at the joints. Cut each one into thigh and drumstick. Slice off the breasts and cut each one in half. Put on a heatproof plate and keep them warm. Reserve the carcass to make a stock for another occasion.

Spoon off all but about 2 tablespoons of the fat from the roasting pan into a heatproof container and keep for another occasion. Add the drained sauerkraut to the fat in the pan and mix well. Pile it all onto a large serving dish, add the heated frankfurters and the pieces of duck with its juices, then serve.

crispy roast duck with Asian greens

Rubbing kosher salt over the duck draws excess moisture out of the skin, while scalding makes for a crispy skin when roasted. A wonderful honey-spiced glaze adds a vibrant colour and flavour to the meat.

1 fresh duck, 1.4 kg/3 lb. 3 oz.

3 tablespoons kosher salt

honey glaze

4 star anise, crushed

100 ml//⅓ cup honey

1 teaspoon ground cinnamon

finely grated zest of 1 orange and freshly squeezed juice of ½ orange (reserve both orange halves for stuffing the duck)

1 teaspoon Sichuan crushed peppercorns

2 tablespoons soy sauce

2.5-cm/1-inch piece fresh ginger, grated

2 red Thai chillies/chiles, chopped

2 tablespoons dark brown sugar

Asian greens

3 tablespoons peanut oil

2 tablespoons toasted sesame oil

2 tablespoons red wine vinegar

1 teaspoon soy sauce

1 teaspoon honey

350 g/scant 5 cups mixed salad greens

cracked black pepper and green tea salt

serves 4

Wash and dry the duck. Rub the kosher salt all over the duck skin, cover, and leave in the refrigerator overnight.

Put the roasting rack on the lined roasting pan. Bring a kettle of water to the boil. Put the duck in a large bowl and pour boiling water over it. Immediately remove the duck from the bowl and place on the roasting rack in the roasting pan. Set aside.

Preheat the oven to 200°C (400°F) Gas 6.

Stuff the duck with the orange halves. Mix all the Honey Glaze ingredients together in a bowl and brush over the duck. Roast in the preheated oven for 30 minutes, remove from the oven, and drain off the fat that has accumulated in the bottom of the pan. You may need to cover the tips of the wings with kitchen foil, as they will be very crispy. Turn the oven down to 190°C (375°F) Gas 5 and put the duck back in the oven for another 30 minutes.

Remove the duck from the oven and leave it to rest for 15 minutes in a warm place.

To prepare the Asian Greens, whisk the peanut oil, sesame oil, red wine vinegar, soy sauce and honey together. Season with the cracked black pepper and green tea salt. Put the salad greens in a bowl and toss with the dressing.

Carve the duck and serve with the salad.

roast duck with cherry salsa

For this dish, choose a breed of duck that is as lean as possible and save any fat rendered during cooking for roasting the potatoes. The breed will depend on where you live, but often will be one crossed with a wild or Barbary duck. For some reason, the Chinese seem to have a monopoly on the best ducks, so if you live near a Chinatown market, buy a fresh duck from there. Serve with Roast Potatoes.

1 duck, about 3 kg

250 ml/1 cup fresh duck or chicken stock

salt (see method)

3 tablespoons clear honey

1 tablespoon red wine vinegar

500 g/1 lb. fresh cherries

1 recipe Cherry Salsa (page 231)

Roast Potatoes (page 170), to serve

an instant-read thermometer

serves 4

Prick the duck all over, especially around the thighs, to release the fat during cooking. Dry with a cloth and rub with salt. Put the duck on its side in a roasting pan and cook in a preheated oven at 250°C (500°F) Gas 9 for 20 minutes. Turn it onto its other side and cook for another 20 minutes, then lower the temperature to 180°C (350°F) Gas 4. Pour off the fat into a heatproof container, let cool, cover and keep in the refrigerator for future roasting.

To make a honey glaze, put the honey and vinegar in a small saucepan and bring to the boil. Boil for 30 seconds, remove from the heat and set aside.

If you are using a roasting rack, set it in the roasting pan. Put the duck on the rack on its back and roast for 40 minutes. Brush the duck with a layer of honey glaze and roast for another 20 minutes. Lift the duck onto a platter and transfer all the pan juices and fat to a saucepan.

Raise the oven temperature to 230°C (450°F) Gas 8. Brush the duck again with glaze, then return it to the oven. Cook for a further 20 minutes or until an instant-read thermometer registers 82°C (180°F) at the thickest part of the thigh.

To make a sauce, remove and discard the duck fat from the sediment in the saucepan, add the stock, taste and reduce if necessary. Carve the duck and serve with the cherry salsa and some roast potatoes.

Scandinavian roast goose

Many Scandinavians celebrate Christmas on Christmas Eve, often with roast goose or duck. The traditional accompaniments for this bird are the apples and prunes used to stuff the goose, plus red cabbage cooked with a tart berry juice such as blackcurrant, plus sugar-glazed potatoes. The combination of rich meat, fruit, plus tart and sweet vegetables is common in many cuisines.

1 goose, about 6 kg/13 lb.

250 g/1½ cups pitted prunes

500 g/1 lb. 2 oz. tart apples, peeled, cored and quartered

75 ml/5 tablespoons red wine

1 tablespoon cornflour/cornstarch, mixed with 1 tablespoon water

150–300 ml/⅔–1⅓ cup chicken stock

3–4 tablespoons cream

sea salt and freshly ground black pepper

to serve

boiled potatoes browned in sugar

sweet pickles

Danish Red Cabbage (page 217)

an instant-read thermometer

serves 6

Dry the goose inside and out with kitchen paper, then rub with salt and pepper and prick the skin all over with a skewer or sharp-pronged fork.

Scald the prunes with boiling water and stuff the goose with the apples and prunes. Rub the skin with salt.

Put the goose breast up on a rack in a roasting pan. Put in a cold oven, turn to 170°C (325°F) Gas 3 and roast for 45 minutes. Add a little cold water to the pan and roast for 3½ hours or according to size (see chart page 19). Take care not to let the water dry up – add extra as necessary. The goose is done when an instant-read thermometer reaches 82°C (180°F). Alternatively, the juices should run clear when you prick the leg at the thickest part. Waggle the leg bone a little – it should move in the socket. Transfer the bird to a platter.

Lift all but 2 tablespoons of fat from the pan into a gravy separator. Pour the gravy juices into a small bowl and stir in the cornflour/cornstarch mixture (keep the goose fat for another use). Increase the oven temperature to 250°C (500°F) Gas 9. Return the goose to the roasting pan, pour 2 tablespoons cold water over the breast and return the bird to the oven.

Pour the wine into a saucepan, add 1 tablespoon of the goose fat, bring to the boil and reduce until syrupy. Add the gravy juices mixture and the stock and return to the boil, stirring. Season well with salt and pepper and stir in the cream.

Carve the goose and serve with the gravy, boiled potatoes browned in sugar, sweet pickles and Danish red cabbage.

game

roasted pheasant breasts with bacon, shallots and mushrooms

Depending on size, you may need two pheasant breasts per person – this is something you can decide when shopping. The look-and-choose, visual method is always best. If you are offered a choice between hen and cock pheasant, buy the hen – they have better breast meat and are plumper. Cooking a whole pheasant is more economical and will serve 2–3 people, but it involves all that last-minute carving and it never looks as good.

6 plump pheasant breasts

12 slices smoked bacon

6 sprigs of thyme

3 fresh bay leaves, halved

25 g/2 tablespoons butter

1 tablespoon olive oil

12 shallots

100 ml/½ cup dry sherry

6 portobello mushrooms, quartered

6 thick slices French bread

200 g/scant 3 cups watercress

sea salt and freshly cracked black pepper

serves 6

Remove the skin from the pheasant breasts and discard it. Wrap 2 slices of bacon around each breast, inserting a sprig of thyme and half a bay leaf between the pheasant and the bacon.

Put the butter and oil into a large roasting pan and set on top of the stove over high heat. Add the pheasant breasts, shallots, sherry, mushrooms, salt and pepper. Turn the pheasant breasts in the mixture until they are well coated. Cook at the top of a preheated oven at 190°C (375°F) Gas 5 for 25 minutes. Remove from the oven and let rest for 5 minutes. Put the bread onto plates, then add the watercress, mushrooms, shallots and pheasant. Spoon over any cooking juices and serve.

boned, rolled and stuffed pheasant breasts with whisky

This delicious recipe is perfect for entertaining. If you have the legs of the pheasant as well as the breasts, use them to make a stock. Otherwise, use good quality chicken stock available from most supermarkets.

4 boneless pheasant breasts

50 g/3½ tablespoons unsalted butter

3 tablespoons whisky

300 ml/1¼ cups chicken or pheasant stock

1 tablespoon cornflour/cornstarch

sea salt and freshly ground black pepper

whisky stuffing

50 g/1¾ oz. onions, chopped

50 g/⅓ cup sultanas/golden raisins

50 g/¼ cup dates, pitted, washed, dried and chopped

60 g/4 tablespoons unsalted butter, plus 2 tablespoons extra, for basting

6 tablespoons whisky

1½ tablespoons cider vinegar

to serve

sautéed potatoes

Roast Apples and Celeriac (page 186)

Cranberry Relish (page 230)

a piping bag (optional)

cocktail sticks

an instant-read thermometer

serves 4

To make the stuffing, remove the fillets from the pheasant breasts and chop them into small pieces, discarding any sinew. Put the onions, sultanas/golden raisins, dates, butter and whisky in a saucepan, bring to the boil, reduce the heat and cook gently until all the liquid has been absorbed. Add the chopped fillets, stir in the vinegar and bring to the boil. Season with salt and pepper, cool and spoon the stuffing into a piping bag, if using.

Rub the breasts with 25 g/2 tablespoons of the butter, salt and pepper, roll them into a loose cylinder and secure with a cocktail stick. Holding them in the palm of your hand, pipe the stuffing into the centres or fill them with a spoon. Turn them over so they are skin side up. Set them, side by side, in a roasting pan and roast in a preheated oven at 250°C (500°F) Gas 9 for 20 minutes until firm, or when an instant-read thermometer registers 82°C (180°F). Remove from the oven and transfer to a serving dish.

Heat the roasting pan on top of the stove, add the whisky and stir and scrape up all the delicious sediment. Bring to the boil, then simmer for a few minutes to drive off the alcohol. Add the stock, remaining butter and cornflour/cornstarch to the pan, stir well, bring to the boil and let bubble for a couple of minutes to thicken it. Pour the juices around the pheasant breasts. Serve on a bed of sautéed potatoes with the roasted apples and celeriac and cranberry relish.

pheasant roasted with vin santo, grapes and walnuts

This is a wonderful Tuscan way to cook pheasant or guinea fowl when the walnuts are falling off the tree and the grapes are bursting with flavour, also in season are little oranges that are green on the outside, but orange and sweet on the inside.

6 unwaxed clementines or other small oranges

675 g/1 lb. 8 oz. white or red grapes, plus extra to garnish

20 fresh walnuts in shell, or 125 g/1¼ cups halved walnuts

30 g dried porcini mushrooms, soaked in warm water for 30 minutes

200 ml/¾ cup Vin Santo

2 young pheasants, plucked, drawn and trussed with giblets

softened butter, for basting

2 teaspoons balsamic vinegar

sea salt and freshly ground black pepper

serves 6

Grate the zest from 2 clementines and squeeze the juice from all of them, then place in a bowl, reserving the ungrated squeezed halves. Purée the grapes roughly in a food processor and pour into the clementine juice. Shell the fresh walnuts.

Strain the mushrooms, reserve liquid and finely chop the mushrooms. Pour half the clementine and grape juice into a roasting pan, adding the Vin Santo and any giblets, except the liver. Put the reserved clementine halves inside the pheasant cavities. Spread the pheasants with butter and season with salt and pepper. Put the birds in the roasting pan on one side, legs uppermost. Roast in a preheated oven at 200ºC (400ºF) Gas 6 for 15 minutes. Turn the birds over on the other side, baste with the pan juices and roast for another 15 minutes. Finally sit the birds upright, baste well and roast for a final 15 minutes or until done. Test by pushing a skewer into the meatiest part of the thigh – the juices should run clear.

Transfer the pheasants to a warmed serving platter and keep warm. Pour the reserved clementine and grape juice into the roasting pan. Stir in the reserved mushroom water, mushrooms and balsamic vinegar. Bring to the boil, scraping up any sediment from the bottom of the roasting pan. Boil for 1–2 minutes, then strain into a saucepan, pressing the juice through the sieve/strainer with the back of a wooden spoon. Stir in the walnuts, bring to the boil and reduce the sauce to 450 ml/scant 2 cups. Taste and season well. The sauce should be slightly syrupy. Spoon the walnuts around the pheasant and garnish with grapes. Serve with the sauce.

guinea fowl with lentils

If you can find a true guinea fowl, from a butcher or specialist supplier, then this will taste as it should. It is worth the effort to search out the real thing because supermarket guinea fowl is disappointing, to say the least. Cooked with white wine, bacon, thyme and bay, the lentils make a hearty and delicious accompaniment to the succulent guinea fowl – a perfect meal to enjoy with the family on a cold day.

1 guinea fowl, about 1.5 kg/3 lb. 5 oz.

3 tablespoons extra virgin olive oil

225 g/1¼ cups dried green lentils, preferably French

a sprig of thyme

1 fresh bay leaf

4 large shallots, chopped

2 carrots, chopped

150 g/⅔ cup bacon lardons

250 ml/1 cup dry white wine

coarse sea salt and freshly ground black pepper

a roasting pan fitted with a rack

serves 4

Rub the guinea fowl all over with 1 tablespoon of the olive oil and season, inside and out. Put on a rack set in a roasting pan and cook in a preheated oven at 220°C (425°F) Gas 7 until browned and the juices run clear when the thigh is pierced with a skewer, about 1 hour.

Meanwhile, put the lentils, thyme and bay leaf into a saucepan and just cover with water. Bring to the boil, reduce the heat, cover with a lid and simmer gently until tender, about 25 minutes. Drain and season with ½ teaspoon salt.

Heat the remaining 2 tablespoons oil in a frying pan/skillet. Add the shallots and carrots and cook until just tender, 3–5 minutes. Stir in the bacon lardons and cook, stirring, until well browned. Add the wine and cook over high heat until reduced by half. Add the lentils, discard the herbs and set aside.

Remove the guinea fowl from the oven and let stand for 10 minutes. Carve into serving pieces and serve immediately, with the lentils.

Italian roast guinea fowl with new potatoes and green beans

Roast guinea fowl is a treat; half chicken, half game, it is full of flavour. Where we might roast whole birds and quite large pieces, Italians tend to cut poultry and meat into small pieces that roast very quickly and absorb other ingredients more directly, giving great finger-licking potential. This recipe makes for a quick, easy and exotic roast to serve for a special meal. Adding the ready-boiled potatoes and beans to the meat in the cooking pan and mixing them up means that none of the meat juices will be wasted.

1.5 kg/3 lb. 5 oz. guinea fowl

30 g/2 tablespoons butter

750 g/1 lb. 10 oz. new potatoes

200 g/1⅓ cups green beans

100 ml/⅓ cup vegetable stock

sea salt

serves 4–6

If using a whole guinea fowl, cut in half lengthways, then cut each half into 6 evenly sized pieces.

Arrange the guinea fowl in a large roasting pan, dot with butter and sprinkle generously with salt. Cover with aluminium foil and leave to stand at room temperature for 1 hour. Remove the foil, put the pan in the middle of a preheated oven and roast at 200°C (400°F) Gas 6 for 30 minutes or until golden brown and tender, turning at least once.

Meanwhile, put the potatoes in a small saucepan of salted water and boil until tender, then drain. Cook the beans in the same way for about 8 minutes, then drain.

Add the potatoes and beans to the roasting dish and stir well to coat with the pan juices. Transfer the meat and vegetables to a serving plate.

Deglaze the roasting pan with the stock, boil until reduced by half, then pour over the meat and vegetables. Serve with radicchio plumes.

Variation Free-range chicken or rabbit are also good cooked in this simple, quick and delicious way.

pot-roasted game bird with apple, cabbage, juniper and cream

A cross between a roast and a stew, you can put this dish in the oven, set the timer, and forget about it. This method keeps the bird moist and tender so the meat will fall from the bones, just the way you want it.

1 game bird, such as pheasant or guinea fowl, or a chicken, well seasoned

3 tablespoons olive oil

50 g/3 tablespoons butter

8 small pickling onions or shallots

2 garlic cloves, crushed

8 juniper berries, crushed

200 ml/¾ cup dry cider

150 ml/⅔ cup good chicken stock

8 baby apples or 4 large, cored and quartered

greens such as the outer leaves of a Savoy cabbage, red brussels tops or black cabbage, separated into leaves, thick ribs removed

150 ml/⅔ cup double/heavy cream

salt and freshly ground black pepper

serves 4

Heat the oil and half the butter in a large frying pan, add the bird and brown it on all sides. Transfer to a deep snug-fitting flameproof casserole dish.

Wipe the pan, then add the remaining butter, onions, garlic and juniper and sauté gently for 2 minutes. Pour in the cider and stock. Simmer for 5 minutes. Add the apples and transfer to the casserole dish.

Heat to simmering, cover with a lid, then transfer to a preheated oven and cook at 180ºC (350ºF) Gas 4 for 45 minutes.

Blanch the cabbage leaves in boiling water for 3 minutes, then tuck the leaves around the bird, pour over the cream, return to the oven and cook for a further 15 minutes. Remove from the oven, cut the bird into portions and serve with the apple, cabbage and juices.

roast rabbit with herbs and cider

A rabbit has to be young if it is to be roasted. Only the very young ones should be roasted whole, giving the most tender pure white meat imaginable. Otherwise it is best to cut the meat into pieces, frying the legs in butter first to give them a bit of colour, then roasting them with the saddle. Some supermarkets sell prepared rabbit pieces – you will need about 1 kg/2 lb. 4 oz. Feel free to use fresh chicken stock, either homemade or from the supermarket, if using these.

4 wild rabbits, about 500 g/1 lb. 2 oz. each or 2 farmed ones

1 onion, chopped

1 carrot, sliced

1 bay leaf

12 slices streaky bacon

100 g/7 tablespoons butter

3 tip sprigs of rosemary, or 1 long one, broken into 3, or 1 teaspoon dried rosemary

6–8 tip sprigs of thyme, 2–3 whole sprigs or ½ teaspoon dried thyme

200 ml/scant 1 cup cider

2 tablespoons double/heavy cream (optional)

sea salt and freshly ground black pepper

an instant-read thermometer

serves 4

First cut the legs and saddle off each rabbit and reserve with the kidneys. To make a stock, put the bones in a saucepan, add the onion, carrot and bay leaf, cover with water and simmer for 1 hour. Strain and reserve the stock, discard the bones, and reserve the onion and carrot.

Loosen the tough membrane around the saddles by sliding the point of a sharp knife along the backbone from under the neck end to the tail, freeing the meat underneath. Do one side at a time, then cut off and discard it. Cover the saddle with strips of bacon.

Melt the butter in a frying pan, add the legs and fry for about 5 minutes to give them a bit of colour. Season with salt, pepper, rosemary and thyme. Put the reserved onion and carrot in a roasting pan and set the legs and saddle on top. Roast in the middle of a preheated oven at 230°C (450°F) Gas 8 for 15–20 minutes according to size or until an instant-read thermometer registers 70°C (160°F).

Meanwhile, add the kidneys to the pan used to brown the legs, adding a little extra butter if necessary. Fry gently until firm, then remove and set aside until serving. Deglaze the pan with the cider, add the stock and the cream, if using, and reduce the gravy to increase the flavour and thicken it. Add salt and pepper to taste.

Arrange the meat a on a serving dish and pour the sauce over the top. Garnish with a sprig of thyme and serve.

marinated roast venison

Saddle of venison, wild or farmed, is almost always tender, and so is the haunch when taken from a young one, but it is still a good idea to tenderize the meat further by hanging it for a while. A good butcher will often do this for you.

1 venison saddle, about 2 kg/4 lb. 8 oz., boned and rolled

stock

½ onion, chopped

250 ml/1 cup red wine

marinade

60 g/4 tablespoons softened butter or 4 tablespoons olive oil

12 juniper berries, crushed

½ teaspoon dried thyme

2 garlic cloves, crushed

5 salted anchovies, well rinsed, then chopped

1 tablespoon port

a strip of pork fat or 3 slices streaky bacon, made into long rolls

3 sprigs of rosemary

sea salt and freshly ground black pepper

gravy

1 tablespoon redcurrant jelly

1 tablespoon cornflour/cornstarch, mixed with 125 ml/½ cup water

pan-fried button mushrooms, to serve

kitchen string

kitchen foil or greaseproof paper

an instant-read thermometer

serves 8–10

Open the saddle and cut away all the loose trimmings from around the rib area and any excess flank, leaving enough to wrap around the meat. To make a stock, put the trimmings, onion, red wine and 500 ml water in a saucepan. Bring to the boil, reduce the heat and simmer gently for 1 hour.

To make the marinade, put the butter or oil, juniper berries, thyme, garlic, anchovies, salt and pepper in a bowl and mix well. Rub the opened saddle with half the marinade and sprinkle with the port, arrange the pork fat or bacon lengthways along the backbone cavity, top with the sprigs of rosemary, close the meat up and tie it with string. Rub the outside with the rest of the marinade, wrap the meat in foil or greaseproof paper and leave in a cool place for at least 3 hours.

Unwrap the meat and put it in a preheated oven at 250°C (450°F) Gas 7 for 10 minutes, then reduce to 170°C (325°F) Gas 3 for 45 minutes or until an instant-read thermometer registers 65°C (150°F). Baste the meat with the pan juices 2–3 times during this period. Transfer the meat to a serving dish and keep it warm, discarding the string. The temperature will continue to rise to 70°C (160°F).

To make the gravy, put the roasting pan on the top of the stove. Add the redcurrant jelly and stock and let it boil until the jelly dissolves, then add the cornflour mixture, return to the boil, season with salt and pepper and add the juices from the pan. Serve the gravy in a jug/pitcher.

Carve the meat straight across the grain, not lengthways as is often done with a saddle. Serve with pan-fried brown button mushrooms.

fish

tuna with paprika crumbs and romesco sauce

Tuna is a dark-fleshed fish that needs extra flavouring and takes well to hot paprika seasoning. The topping gives a moist and crunchy texture to a fish that can become dry and overcooked only too easily. Serve on a bed of buttered spinach with romesco sauce – a hot, pungent, Catalan sauce thickened with ground almonds and hazelnuts, which is often served with fish and can also be used as a dip for crudités.

4 tuna steaks, 175 g/6 oz. each

40 g/1½ oz. Cheddar cheese, cut into 4 thin slices

sea salt and freshly ground black pepper

paprika breadcrumb crunch

1 tablespoon olive oil

50 g/1 cup fresh white breadcrumbs

1 tablespoon chopped fresh basil

½ teaspoon hot oak-smoked paprika

1 teaspoon tomato paste

½ teaspoon sugar

½ teaspoon salt

to serve

Romesco Sauce (page 231)

serves 4

To make the paprika topping, put the oil in a frying pan/skillet, add the breadcrumbs, basil, paprika, tomato paste, sugar and salt. Stir well and fry until crunchy. Remove from the pan and let cool.

Season the tuna with salt and pepper, put on the oiled baking tray and roast in a preheated oven at 250°C (500°F) Gas 9 for 5 minutes.

Remove from the oven and turn over the steaks. Pile the paprika breadcrumbs on top, then add the slice of cheese. Return to the oven and cook for a further 5 minutes or until the cheese has melted. Serve with romesco sauce.

tuna steaks baked with rosemary

Tuna is a very filling and rich fish. Although one never thinks of cooking it with rosemary, it is a marriage made in heaven – especially when flavoured with good olive oil and some capers to cut the richness.

4 x 150 g/5 oz. tuna steaks

2 tablespoons chopped fresh rosemary, plus extra sprigs to garnish (optional)

1 tablespoon salted capers, rinsed and dried and chopped

4 tablespoons dry white wine

4 tablespoons extra virgin olive oil

sea salt and freshly ground black pepper

lemon wedges, to serve

serves 4

Coat the tuna steaks with the rosemary. Transfer each steak onto a big square of baking parchment or kitchen foil. Scatter the capers on top then pour the wine over. Season well with salt and pepper, then drizzle with olive oil. Loosely but securely twist or close the paper or foil around the tuna – it should be loose enough to fill with steam as it cooks, but secure enough not to let the juices escape during the cooking.

Bake in a preheated oven at 180ºC (350ºF) Gas 4 for 15 minutes. Serve each packet on a hot plate for each diner to open for themselves, with lemon wedges and garnished with rosemary sprigs, if liked.

roasted Provençal salmon and vegetables with rouille

Bright and festive, the colours and aromas in this dish will transport you to the south of France. Be sure to choose a wrinkly, gutsy black olive for this dish; ordinary pitted black olives simply won't do. This is ideal for both informal dining or entertaining and in either case you can serve it straight from the roasting pan.

500 g/1 lb. baby new potatoes, scrubbed and quartered

500 g/1 lb. courgettes/zucchinis, halved and quartered

1 fennel bulb, halved and sliced

1 red bell pepper, cored, deseeded and sliced

1 yellow bell pepper, cored, deseeded and sliced

3 plum tomatoes, cored and quartered

2 red onions, sliced into sixths

a good pinch of saffron threads

a few sprigs of fresh thyme

4–5 tablespoons olive oil

120 g/1 cup pitted black olives, halved

a small handful of fresh basil leaves, shredded

4 boneless, skinless salmon fillets (about 150 g/5 oz. each)

sea salt and freshly ground black pepper

for the rouille

200 ml/¾ cup fresh mayonnaise

2–4 garlic cloves, crushed

½ teaspoon paprika

a pinch of cayenne pepper

serves 4

Preheat the oven to 220ºC (425ºF) Gas 7.

Combine all of the vegetables in a large roasting pan. Add the saffron and thyme and a good dose of the olive oil. Toss with your hands to coat evenly. Spread the vegetables out in an even layer and sprinkle with salt.

Bake in the preheated oven for 25–30 minutes, until just browned.

Meanwhile, prepare the rouille. Combine all the ingredients in a small bowl, adding garlic and cayenne to taste. Mix well, adjust the seasoning if necessary and set aside.

Remove the vegetables from the oven and sprinkle over the olives and basil. Arrange the salmon on top, drizzle a little of the olive oil over each fillet and season with salt and pepper. Return to the oven and bake for about 15 minutes more, until the salmon is just cooked through. Serve immediately, with the rouille on the side for spooning.

roast salmon fillets with sorrel sauce

Years ago, one of the most popular ways to cook salmon was to poach it either as cutlets or whole. However, now that salmon is more often filleted, the best way to cook it is to roast skin side up, then peel off the skin and scales as soon as it is cooked. This way, there is no messy draining of the fish and less chance of overcooking it – salmon being one fish that's best served slightly rare. If you cannot easily get sorrel, season the sauce with lemon juice instead.

4 salmon fillets or tranches, about 175 g/ 6 oz. each

3 tablespoons plain/all-purpose flour, seasoned with salt and pepper

unsalted butter, for roasting

sorrel sauce

125 g/1 stick plus 2 tablespoons unsalted butter

60 g/2 oz. sorrel leaves

3 egg yolks

sea salt and freshly ground black pepper

to serve

Fennel Roasted in Butter (page 182)

boiled new potatoes

serves 4

Heat the buttered baking sheet in a preheated oven at 230°C (450°F) Gas 8. Dust the fillets with the flour and put them skin side up on the sheet. Roast for 6–8 minutes. Test for doneness by trying to remove the skin – if it comes off, the fish is ready.

Remove from the oven, then carefully peel off the skin and discard it. Keep the fish warm.

To make the sorrel sauce, put the butter in a saucepan and heat until it begins to froth. Add the sorrel and simmer until it turns a khaki colour. Put the egg yolks in a blender, add 2 tablespoons water and blend until fluffy. Reduce the speed and pour all the sorrel and butter into the egg mixture with the machine running. Taste and adjust the seasoning with salt and pepper.

Spoon pools of sauce onto 4 heated dinner plates. Turn the fillets over onto the sauce and serve with roast fennel and new potatoes.

baked trout stuffed with dates

Cooking fish with dates is a lovely Moroccan tradition. Trout and shad are often selected for this dish, which can be cooked in a tagine on the stove or in the oven. Cooking fish in this manner is often reserved for banquets and family celebrations where the whole fish is displayed with dates stuffed with almond paste.

4 small or 2 large fresh trout, gutted, rinsed and patted dry

3 tablespoons olive oil with a pat of butter, or 2 tablespoons ghee

1 onion, finely chopped

25 g/2-inch piece of fresh ginger, peeled and finely chopped

2–3 teaspoons ground cinnamon plus 1 teaspoon for dusting

2–3 tablespoons blanched almonds, finely chopped

100 g/½ cup medium- or short-grain rice, rinsed and drained

200 g/6½ oz. moist, ready-to-eat dates, chopped

a small bunch of fresh coriander/cilantro leaves, finely chopped

a small bunch of fresh flat leaf parsley, finely chopped

1 orange, cut into thin slices

sea salt and freshly ground black pepper

serves 4

Preheat the oven to 180ºC (350ºF) Gas 4. Using a sharp knife, slit the trout open along the belly and season the cavities with salt and pepper. Line an ovenproof dish with plenty of foil, so that the fish can be wrapped in it, and place the fish side by side on the foil.

Heat most of the oil and butter or ghee in a heavy-based saucepan. Stir in the onion and ginger and cook for 2–3 minutes, until they begin to colour. Stir in the cinnamon and almonds, add the rice and season to taste with salt and pepper. Pour in just enough water to cover the rice and bring it to the boil. Reduce the heat and simmer gently until all the water has been absorbed. Turn off the heat, cover the pan and leave the rice to steam for 10 minutes.

Add the dates, coriander/cilantro and parsley to the rice and let it cool before stuffing the fish with it. To do this, spoon the filling into the cavities and brush the tops of the fish with the remaining oil or ghee. Place the orange slices around the fish, wrap up the foil to form a package, and place the dish in the preheated oven for 15–20 minutes. Open the foil and bake for a further 5 minutes, to lightly brown the top. Decorate the fish with a thin line of ground cinnamon by rubbing it between your thumb and index finger. Serve immediately.

marinated sea bass with paprika and spices

Roasting brings out the best in sea bass, firming up the flesh and concentrating its flavour. Because it is now farmed, there should be no shortage of this splendid fish – small, one-portion bass should always be available. However, the dish is even better if you can find a large, 2 kg wild one. This vivid sauce may be made in advance – serve it separately in a jug.

1 large (2 kg/4–5 lb.) or 4 small (500 g/ 1 lb. each) sea bass, scaled and cleaned

sea salt and freshly ground black pepper

marinade

freshly squeezed juice of 2 lemons

2 tablespoons olive oil

½ teaspoon ground cumin

1 teaspoon sweet oak-smoked paprika

sauce

2 red bell peppers

2 tablespoons olive oil

½ teaspoon cumin

1 teaspoon sweet oak-smoked paprika

1 garlic clove, crushed

8 medium tomatoes, skinned, deseeded and chopped

a pinch of saffron threads, infused in 125 ml/½ cup boiling water

125 ml/½ cup red wine vinegar

1 teaspoon salt

1 teaspoon sugar

1 tablespoon chopped fresh flat leaf parsley

an instant-read thermometer

serves 4

To make the marinade, put the lemon juice, olive oil, cumin and paprika in a bowl and beat with a fork.

Cover a baking sheet with non-stick parchment, to act as a cradle when you are ready to lift the fish onto a serving dish.

Cut off the fins, check the cavities and rinse out only if necessary. Pat dry with paper towels, then brush the cavities with some of the marinade and reserve the rest. Put the fish on the parchment, cover with a damp cloth and leave for 2 hours in a cool place.

Meanwhile, to make the sauce, roast the bell peppers in a preheated oven at 220°C (425°F) Gas 7 until the skins start to char and they can be peeled. Remove from the heat, remove the skins, pull out the stalks and discard the seeds and white membrane. Cut the flesh into small chunks and set aside.

Heat the remaining marinade in a small pan, add the oil, cumin, paprika and garlic and cook gently for a couple of minutes until aromatic. Add the tomatoes, saffron, vinegar, salt and sugar and cook to a purée. Add the bell peppers and parsley and reheat thoroughly, without boiling, otherwise the sauce will lose some of its freshness.

Season the fish with salt and pepper, put it (still in its parchment cradle) in a roasting pan and cook in a preheated oven at 220°C (425°F) Gas 7 for 25–30 minutes or until an instant-read thermometer registers 58°C (136°F) at the thickest part of the back. Smaller fish will take about 20 minutes. Transfer to a large dish, remove the parchment and serve the sauce in a small jug.

sea bass baked in parchment

Sea bass has a wonderful, clean, fresh taste and cooking in parchment is the best way to cook whole fish (with the possible exception of grilling over embers). The parchment lets the fish steam in its own juices, absorbing the aroma of the fresh herbs and lemon. This cooking time should be perfect – the fish is better slightly underdone at the bone than overdone. The packets should be opened at the table to appreciate the full aroma.

2 sea bass, about 350 g/12 oz. each, cleaned and scaled

about 1 tablespoon olive oil

4 fresh bay leaves

2 sprigs of thyme

6 thin slices of lemon

about 2 tablespoons dry white wine or freshly squeezed lemon juice

sea salt and freshly ground black pepper

serves 2

Cut 2 large rectangles of baking parchment big enough to wrap each fish generously. Brush the rectangles with a little oil.

Season the cavities of the fish with salt and pepper. Put 2 bay leaves in each one and tuck in the thyme and lemon slices.

Put one fish on one half of the paper, sprinkle with white wine or lemon juice, fold over the other half loosely and twist or fold the edges tightly together to seal. Repeat with the other fish, then put both packets on the baking tray.

Bake in a preheated oven at 190°C (375°F) Gas 5 for 20 minutes. Serve immediately, opening the packets at the table.

oven-roasted red snapper with sorrel and salsa verde

This recipe may be used with any round fish, but preferably not an oily variety. The sorrel is not essential, but it does supply a lemony seasoning for the dish. Serve with roast tomatoes and new potatoes.

4 red snapper, about 500 g/1 lb. each, scaled and cleaned

100 g/1 stick unsalted butter

24 sorrel leaves

sea salt and freshly ground black pepper

Salsa Verde (page 231), to serve

an instant-read thermometer

serves 4

Make sure the fish have been well scaled – snapper have very large scales that can be unpleasant if you bite into one.

Cut off the heads, if preferred, season the cavities with salt and pepper, then butter very well. Arrange the sorrel on the buttered baking sheet and put the fish on top. Lay some more leaves over the fish and roast them in a preheated oven at 250°C (500°F) Gas 9 for 8 minutes. Turn them over and cook for a further 8 minutes, or until an instant-read thermometer registers 58°C (136°F).

Remove the fish from the oven and transfer to heated dinner plates. Warm the salsa verde and trickle over the fish.

roast cod cutlets on a base of thyme and lemon

A very versatile dish, this can be served just as it is or made into a special-occasion, all-in-one dish with one of the sauces. Prepared in advance, it needs only to be roasted, basted and served for an effortless supper.

6 cod cutlets, 250 g/8 oz. each for a main course, 200 g/7 oz. as a starter

about 2 tablespoons unsalted butter

freshly grated nutmeg

6 lemon slices

2 large potatoes, par-boiled in salted water and cut into walnut-sized pieces

sea salt and freshly ground black pepper

base of thyme and lemon

175 g/1 stick plus 5 tablespoons unsalted butter

2 onions, chopped

2 garlic cloves, crushed

1 teaspoon fresh lemon thyme leaves

6 peppercorns

2 bay leaves

to serve (optional)

tomato sauce, such as Romesco (page 231)

Fennel Roasted in Butter (page 182)

serves 6

Season the cutlets with sea salt and freshly ground black pepper.

To make the base of thyme and lemon, heat the butter in a frying pan/skillet, add the onions, garlic, thyme, peppercorns and bay leaves and cook gently until softened but not browned.

Spread the mixture in a roasting pan. Put the cutlets on top, with about 1 teaspoon of the butter on each piece. Add the nutmeg and lemon slices. Tuck the potato pieces around. Roast in a preheated oven at 190°C (375°F) Gas 5 for 35 minutes, basting once with the juices from the lemon slices.

Serve as it is, or with a tomato and roast fennel.

whole roast monkfish

Roasting fish instead of the usual meat joint or bird can make a wonderful change, and makes a lighter roast, perfect for a summer weekend. This recipe uses a sturdy, meaty monkfish as most other fish would be overwhelmed by the robust flavours in this Provençal preparation. Good fishmongers will make sure the thin grey membrane that lies under the skin is removed; but if it isn't, insist that it is, all the way down the tail, because it's a difficult job to do at home.

1 monkfish tail, about 600 g/18 oz.

about 12 thin slices smoked bacon or prosciutto – enough to cover the fish

2 tablespoons extra virgin olive oil

200 g/7 oz. mushrooms, sliced

2 large garlic cloves, crushed

250 ml/1 cup dry white wine

1 kg/2 lbs. tomatoes, skinned, deseeded and chopped

2 tablespoons crème fraîche or sour cream

a handful of basil leaves, chopped

coarse sea salt and freshly ground black pepper

serves 4

Preheat the oven to 220°C (425°F) Gas 7.

Lay out the bacon on a work surface with the slices slightly overlapping each other. Put the monkfish on top, belly up. Wrap it in the bacon with the ends overlapping across the belly. Turn it over and set aside.

Heat the oil in a large frying pan/skillet. Add the mushrooms and a pinch of salt and cook until browned, about 3–5 minutes. Stir in the garlic, then add the wine and cook over high heat for 1 minute. Stir in the tomatoes, salt lightly and simmer gently for 5 minutes.

Pour this tomato sauce into a baking dish just large enough to hold the fish. Set the fish on top and roast for 15 minutes. Lower the oven temperature to 200°C (400°F) Gas 6 and roast for 30 minutes more. Remove from the oven and put the fish on a plate. Stir the crème fraîche and basil into the tomatoes. Set the monkfish back on top and serve.

vegetables

roast potatoes

Potatoes are the quintessential roasted vegetable. Though new potatoes are used for roasting, the traditional choice is an old, floury potato, such as Maris Piper or King Edward/russet or Idaho. The idea is to get a crisp, crunchy outside and a fluffy inside. Potatoes can be roasted, either peeled or unpeeled and are often par-boiled first. This gives them a fluffier interior and crisper exterior. If you score the outside of the potato first with a fork, they will be extra crunchy. The roasting fat used depends on what part of the world you live in. In some areas, it's olive oil (and increasingly so everywhere, as people get more health-conscious). In much of France and Scandinavia, it is butter. In south-west France, it is often delicious goose fat and duck fat, which undoubtedly give the best flavour.

potatoes roasted in cream

150 ml/⅔ cup double (heavy) cream

½ teaspoon hot dry mustard

½ teaspoon salt

500 g/1 lb. potatoes, peeled and halved

serves 4

Potatoes roasted in cream (right)

Put the cream, mustard and salt in a measuring jug/cup and beat with a fork. Put the potatoes in a small roasting pan and pour the cream mixture over the top. Roast in a preheated oven at 180°C (350°F) Gas 4 for 1 hour, basting every 20 minutes. Serve with roast meat or poultry. The cream becomes buttery as it cooks – don't worry, it's going to turn brown and crumbly.

roast potatoes with bacon and garlic

8 thick slices smoked streaky bacon, cut into squares

2 tablespoons olive oil

3 garlic cloves, sliced (optional)

500 g/1 lb. new potatoes, unpeeled, cut into 1 cm/½-inch chunks

sea salt and freshly ground black pepper

1 tablespoon sliced spring onion tops/scallion greens, to serve

serves 4

Roast potatoes with bacon and garlic

Put the bacon in a roasting pan, pour over the oil and toss to coat. Roast in a preheated oven at 190°C (375°F) Gas 5 for 5 minutes, adding the garlic, if using, after 3 minutes. Add the potatoes and toss to coat with the oil. Season with salt and pepper and roast for 30 minutes, stirring every 10 minutes. Serve sprinkled with the sliced spring onion tops/scallions.

hasselback potatoes

A spectacular recipe from Sweden and one of the crunchiest ways to roast potatoes. It was invented in a Stockholm restaurant, Hasselbacken, which is still open today. It is delicious in that it provides multiple surfaces to become crisp. I have also seen it cooked with fresh bay leaves pressed into the slits (just tell your guests to remove them before eating – bay leaves are wonderful for flavouring, but not for eating).

6 medium roasting potatoes

4 tablespoons butter or goose fat, melted

2 tablespoons sieved and toasted breadcrumbs*

1 tablespoon freshly grated Parmesan cheese

sea salt and freshly ground black pepper

serves 6

Peel the potatoes and slice a thin sliver off each base to make the potato sit steady. Stick a skewer through each one, parallel to the work surface and about 1 cm/½ inch from the base – this will prevent the knife from cutting right through the potato. Cut and slice the potatoes downwards towards the skewer, then remove the skewer. Soak and rinse them in several changes of water to remove the starch, which would stick the slices together.

Season with salt and pepper and sit them in a roasting pan in a preheated oven at 220°C (425°F) Gas 7 to dry off for 2 minutes, then baste with the melted butter.

Return the potatoes to the oven, basting several more times during the cooking until they are brown and crisp, about 1 hour.

Variation Sprinkle with breadcrumbs or cheese at least 30 minutes before the end of the cooking time.

* To make dried breadcrumbs, remove the crusts from a loaf of white bread and pulverize the rest in a blender. Spread the crumbs on a baking sheet and toast in a preheated oven at 250°F (475°F) Gas 9 for 5 minutes until brown on top. Turn them over to expose the white crumb and continue toasting until dry and lightly brown all over. This will take several turns. Shake them through a coarse sieve and discard any residual crumb. Pour into a plastic bag, seal and store in the freezer.

sweet potatoes en brochette

These look rather like hasselback potatoes, except they are skewered right through the centre, then cut around to free each slice, leaving the skewer in place. This browns the slices individually without letting them fall to pieces in the pan. At the same time, they pick up lots of flavour from the roast.

6 smallish sweet potatoes

fat from around the roast or 3 tablespoons goose fat or butter

sea salt and freshly ground black pepper

6 metal skewers

serves 6

Peel the sweet potatoes and skewer each one lengthways through the centre. Slice them around the skewer and separate the rounds.

Arrange them around the bird or meat or in the roasting tin, baste generously with the cooking juices, goose fat or butter and season lightly with salt and pepper.

Roast in a preheated oven at 220°C (425°F) Gas 7 for 45 minutes or until browned – continue to baste them from time to time to prevent them from drying out.

creamy potato gratin

Cream and potatoes, mingling in the heat of the oven, are almost all you'll find in this well-loved dish. If it had cheese, it wouldn't be a true dauphinois. Serve on its own, with a mixed green salad, or as a partner for simple roast meat or poultry.

2 kg /4½ lb. waxy salad-style potatoes, cut into half if large

2 litres/quarts whole milk

1 fresh bay leaf

30 g/2 tablespoons unsalted butter

550 ml/2 cups whipping cream

a pinch of grated nutmeg

coarse sea salt

a baking dish, 30 cm/12 inches long

serves 4–6

Put the potatoes in a large saucepan with the milk and bay leaf. Bring to the boil, then lower the heat, add a pinch of salt and simmer gently until part-cooked, 5–10 minutes.

Drain the potatoes. When cool enough to handle (but still hot), slice into rounds about 3 mm/⅛ inch thick.

Spread the butter in the bottom of the baking dish. Arrange half the potato slices in the dish and sprinkle with salt. Put the remaining potato on top and sprinkle with more salt. Pour in the cream and sprinkle with the grated nutmeg.

Bake in a preheated oven at 180°C (350°F) Gas 4 until golden and the cream is almost absorbed, but not completely, 45 minutes. Serve hot.

glazed roast carrots

So often carrots are used as part of a stew. For them to stand out as a vegetable dish, a little extra attention will make them something special. This treatment makes them sweet and glistening.

750 g/1½ lb. young carrots

1 tablespoon olive oil

50 g/4 tablespoons unsalted butter

1 teaspoon sugar

125 ml/½ cup Madeira wine

sea salt and freshly ground black pepper

a handful of flat leaf parsley, coarsely chopped, to serve

serves 4–6

Wash and trim the carrots. If large, cut into 4 cm/1½-inch chunks, but if small or medium, leave them whole. Parboil them in a large saucepan of boiling water for about 10 minutes, leaving them still slightly hard in the middle. Drain.

Meanwhile, heat the oil and butter in a roasting pan in a preheated oven at 200°C (400°F) Gas 6 until the butter begins to brown. Add the carrots, turn to coat in the oil, then sprinkle with salt, pepper and the sugar and return to the oven for 10 minutes. Turn them and roast for a further 15 minutes. Add the Madeira and cook until all the liquid has gone. Serve sprinkled with parsley.

Variation: Roast carrots with honey and lemon glaze

To make the honey and lemon glaze, put 2 tablespoons honey or sugar in a pan, add 2 tablespoons water, 2 teaspoons lemon juice and 10 g/1 tablespoon butter or 2 teaspoons olive oil. Bring to the boil and simmer for 1 minute to make a light syrup. Start the recipe as above, but pour over the honey and lemon glaze instead of the Madeira. Roast for a further 15 minutes or until the sugar caramelizes. Serve sprinkled with chopped parsley.

carrots with cream and herbs

Thyme is omnipresent in French cuisine. Here, it transforms what would otherwise be ordinary boiled carrots into something subtly sumptuous. The crème fraîche helps too. You can substitute steamed baby leeks for the carrots, but stir in a tablespoon or so of butter when adding the crème fraîche.

800 g/2 lb. baby carrots, trimmed, or medium carrots

50 g/3 tablespoons unsalted butter

a sprig of thyme

2 tablespoons crème fraîche or sour cream

several sprigs of chervil

a small bunch of chives

fine sea salt

serves 4

If using larger carrots, cut them diagonally into 5 cm/2-inch slices. Put in a large saucepan (the carrots should fit in almost a single layer for even cooking). Add the butter and set over low heat. Cook to melt and coat, about 3 minutes. Half fill the saucepan with water, then add a pinch of salt and the thyme. Cover and cook until the water is almost completely evaporated, 10–20 minutes.

Stir in the cream and add salt to taste. Using kitchen scissors, snip the chervil and chives over the top, mix well and serve.

Variation In spring, when turnips are sweet, they make a nice addition to this dish. Peel and quarter large turnips, or just peel baby ones – the main thing is to ensure that all the vegetable pieces (carrot and turnip) are about the same size so that they cook evenly. Halve the carrot quantity and complete with turnips, or double the recipe. Sprinkle with a large handful of just-cooked shelled peas before serving for extra crunch and pretty colour.

fennel roasted in butter

It is a pity that so often this vegetable is just plainly boiled.
Properly blanched for a short while, then roasted in butter,
it is transformed into a perfect accompaniment for any roast,
especially fish.

3 bulbs of Florence fennel

4 tablespoons/¼ cup olive oil or melted butter

sea salt

chopped dill, tarragon or fennel fronds (optional), to serve

serves 6

Trim and remove the stalks/stems and coarse outer leaves
from the fennel if necessary. Cut each bulb in half, then
each half into 2–3 pieces, depending on size. Slice each
piece with a bit of stem or root attached to keep the
pieces in place. Reserve any feathery fronds, to chop over
the dish just before serving.

Put the fennel in a large saucepan of lightly salted water,
bring to the boil and blanch until nearly tender. Drain
and pat dry.

Arrange the pieces in a single layer in a roasting pan,
baste with the oil or butter and cook in a preheated oven
at 220°C (425°F) Gas 7 for about 20 minutes. From time
to time, turn them and baste with the oil or butter so
they brown evenly on all sides.

To enhance the aniseed flavour, dust with chopped dill,
tarragon or fennel fronds, if using, then serve.

Variation Sprinkle with cheese and cook a further
5 minutes, then serve as a separate dish or starter.

braised whole globe artichokes

This is a much better alternative to the usual boiled artichokes, as the bases gently fry in the fragrant oil whilst the leaves steam in the vapour. Florentines use a variety of artichoke known as *mamme* – they are large and sometimes have a baby artichoke attached to the same stalk.

2 lemons, sliced

6 globe artichokes, with stems if possible

100 ml/6 tablespoons extra virgin olive oil, plus extra to serve

sea salt and freshly ground black pepper

serves 6

First prepare the artichokes. Fill a big bowl with water, and add the lemon slices to acidulate it. To prepare the artichokes, starting at the base, snap off all the really tough outer leaves, then snip off the tough tips of the remaining leaves. Slice off the stalks close to the base and put each artichoke in the lemony water until needed to stop them discolouring. Using a potato peeler, peel the stems, dropping them into the water as you go – the stems are just as delicious as the base of the artichokes. Drain the artichokes thoroughly, then turn them upside-down and smack each one lightly with the flat of your hand to slightly separate the leaves. Stand them upright in a large deep saucepan that they will fit snugly in.

Pour the olive oil into the saucepan and set over a medium heat. Season them with salt and pepper and cover the pan. Let them cook for about 15 minutes until the bottoms are nicely browned. Pour in about 150 ml/ ⅔ cup water, bring to the boil, re-cover and simmer very gently for another 20–25 minutes until really tender – a leaf should pull away with little or no resistance. Serve with the pan juices and extra olive oil, salt and pepper.

roast apples and celeriac/celery root or parsnips

Be sure to use a sweet eating apple for this recipe. The cooking variety turns to a purée and spoils the roasting effect. Celeriac/celery root must be thickly peeled to remove the tough outer skin. Choose young celeriac/celery root, because older ones develop a soft, spongy centre, unlike parsnips, which develop woody cores. Ideally, the centres of both vegetables should be cut away before cooking.

2 tablespoons olive oil

½ teaspoon dried sage

½ teaspoon salt

1 eating apple, cut into wedges

1 celeriac/celery root or 2 parsnips, about 350 g/12 oz., peeled and cut into wedges

1 tablespoon chopped fresh flat leaf parsley

serves 4

Put the oil, sage and salt in a plastic bag, then add the apple and celeriac/celery root or parsnips. Roll them around until well coated with oil. Empty the bag onto a baking sheet and roast in a preheated oven at 220°C (425°F) Gas 7 for 30 minutes, turning the vegetables every 10 minutes. Sprinkle with parsley, mix well and serve.

Variations:

Parsnip crisps

Slice 500 g/1 lb. parsnips into thin rounds and coat with olive oil, salt and pepper. Spread them out on a baking sheet and roast until brown and crisp. Serve with any roast meat, especially game.

Roast parsnips

To make one of the traditional accompaniments for roast beef (page 24), peel 500 g/1 lb. parsnips, then cut lengthways into halves or quarters, depending on size. Roast beside the beef for 1–1½ hours or until they develop a caramelized, roasted finish.

roast red onions

These onions are meant to be served in their skins and the centres squeezed or spooned out by the guests. They make a wonderful antipasto, but if you are serving them as a side dish with lamb, insert a sprig of rosemary into the onions before roasting.

12 large red onions

4 tablespoons olive oil

sea salt and freshly ground black pepper

herbed butter

250 g/2 sticks unsalted butter, softened

4 tablespoons chopped fresh herbs, such as thyme, tarragon and/or chives

serves 6–12 as an antipasto

To make the herbed butter, put the softened butter in a bowl and mash with a fork. Add the herbs and mash again. Use from the bowl, or chill a little, transfer to a sheet of kitchen foil and roll into a log. The log may be kept in the refrigerator or frozen for future use. You can cut off rounds to use with dishes such as pan-grilled steak or steamed vegetables.

To prepare the onions, leave their skins on, but take a small slice off each root and trim the ends so they will sit upright. Brush them all over with half the olive oil and cut each one from the top down towards the root without cutting right through. Give them a quarter turn and make a similar cut as before.

Pack them closely into a roasting pan so they sit upright. Open the cuts a little, pour ½ teaspoon of oil into each one, then sprinkle with salt and pepper.

Roast in a preheated oven at 190°C (375°F) Gas 5 for 1½ hours or until the centres are soft. Lift them onto individual plates and put a spoonful of herb butter into each one. Alternatively, pile into a serving dish for guests to help themselves.

Variation Put 4 tablespoons cider vinegar, 4 tablespoons honey, 2 crushed garlic cloves and 1 tablespoon raisins in a saucepan and simmer for 1 minute. Add this to the onions during the last 30 minutes of cooking time.

roast whole heads of garlic with goats' cheese and croutes

You might think that whole roast heads of garlic would would taste a bit robust, but such long cooking renders the cloves sweet, soft and nutty. Press out the flesh and spread it on toasted croutes, then serve in soup, with stews, or with this summery salad.

4 whole heads of garlic

olive oil, plus extra to serve

sea salt and freshly ground black pepper

to serve

bitter leaves, such as frisée, or peppery ones, such as rocket

8 slices goats' cheese, about 2 cm/¾ inch thick

lemon wedges

8 oven-toasted slices of baguette

serves 8 as a starter

Cut each head of garlic in half, then arrange in a single layer in a roasting pan. Spoon olive oil over the top and sprinkle with salt. Roast in a preheated oven at 200°C (400°F) Gas 6 for 45 minutes–1 hour or until the cloves are very soft.

Serve on a bed of bitter leaves with a thick slice of goats' cheese, a wedge of lemon and an oven-toasted croute or slice of bread. Dress with olive oil and freshly ground black pepper. Guests press the garlic paste out of the papery peel and spread it on the croutes. Eat with the cheese and salad leaves.

Variations:

Individually roasted garlic cloves

Arrange the peeled garlic cloves in an ovenproof dish, add 4 tablespoons/¼ cup olive oil and toss until well coated. Roast in a preheated oven at 180°C (350°F) Gas 4 for 30 minutes.

Roast garlic with sugar and brandy

Roast peeled garlic cloves as above for 30 minutes, then sprinkle with 4 tablespoons/¼ cup sugar and 4 tablespoons/¼ cup brandy. Return to the oven for another 30 minutes until they are crunchy.

roast mushrooms with olive oil and pine nuts

Big flat mushrooms are delicious roasted in the oven, and so are the wild ones with an extra touch of hazelnut oil added to the cooking medium. Serve them as a first course, as part of an antipasti selection or as an accompaniment to roast meats, especially beef.

1 tablespoon pine nuts

8 portobello mushrooms, or a mixture with cèpes (porcini), about 350 g/12 oz.

1 tablespoon lemon juice

4 tablespoons/¼ cup olive oil

2 garlic cloves, crushed

sea salt and freshly ground black pepper

1 tablespoon chopped fresh flat leaf parsley, to serve

serves 4 as an accompaniment or 2 as a starter

Put the pine nuts in a dry frying pan/skillet and cook over gentle heat until golden. Shake from time to time and watch them closely because they burn easily. When aromatic, remove them to a plate and set aside.

Wipe or gently brush the mushrooms with a pastry brush to remove any dust, but do not wash them unless absolutely necessary.

Put the lemon juice in a bowl and stir in 3 tablespoons water.

Put the oil, garlic, salt and pepper in a small jug/pitcher or bowl and pour half of it over the base of a large baking sheet.

Arrange the mushrooms on the sheet, open side down, in one layer and brush the tops with the rest of the oil.

Roast in a preheated oven at 220°C (425°F) Gas 7 for 10 minutes, then turn them over with tongs. Brush the inside of the mushrooms with the diluted lemon juice and return them to the oven for a further 5 minutes.

Remove from the oven, sprinkle with the pine nuts and chopped parsley and serve.

stuffed giant mushrooms with feta and herbs

Look out for pine mushrooms in the autumn. They will be foraged and hand-picked by specialists. Cook them whole with as little fuss as possible. Their flavour is best appreciated if they are left to sit for a short while and served warm rather than hot.

8 very large/portobello mushrooms, stalks removed

100 g/4 oz. feta cheese, grated

40 g/2 oz. blanched almonds, roughly chopped

50 g/2 oz. stale white breadcrumbs

1 tablespoon chopped fresh flat leaf parsley

1 tablespoon snipped fresh chives

2 teaspoons olive oil

1 tablespoon chilled butter, finely cubed, plus 2 tablespoons extra

6 baby courgettes/zucchinis, halved lengthways

100 g/4 oz. fine green beans, trimmed

4 small leeks, thinly sliced

65 ml/¼ cup dry white wine

freshly squeezed lemon juice, to taste

sea salt and freshly ground black pepper

serves 4

Preheat the oven to 170°C (325°F) Gas 3.

Sit the mushrooms, gill-side up, in a lightly-oiled baking dish. Put the feta, almonds, breadcrumbs and herbs in a bowl and use your fingers to quickly combine. Stir in the olive oil. Spoon the mixture into the mushrooms and press down gently. Dot the cubed butter over the top. Bake in the preheated oven for about 40–45 minutes, until the mushrooms are really soft and the tops golden.

Meanwhile, bring a saucepan of lightly salted water to the boil. Add the courgettes/zucchinis and beans to the water and cook for 1 minute. Drain well and set aside. About 15 minutes before the mushrooms are cooked, heat the extra butter in a frying pan/skillet set over high heat. Add the leeks and cook for 2 minutes, stirring until softened. Add the courgettes/zucchinis and beans and cook for 2–3 minutes, until tender. Add the wine and cook for 1 minute, until almost all of it has evaporated. Add a squeeze of lemon juice and season well. Arrange the vegetables on a serving plate and sit the mushrooms on top.

crunchy roast garlic tomatoes

When roasted, the flavour of tomatoes becomes more intense because the moisture dries out in the oven. Even so, the better the quality of the tomato to begin with, the better the final dish will be. So buy the Italian varieties, which are often peculiar shapes, but have an extra something when it comes to flavour (what does shape matter when you've been dried out?)

4 large Italian tomatoes

1 teaspoon sugar

4 tablespoons/¼ cup olive oil

25 g/½ cup fresh breadcrumbs

1 garlic clove, crushed

1 tablespoon chopped fresh flat leaf parsley

sea salt

serves 4

Slice the tomatoes in half around the 'equator'. Set them in a roasting dish, sprinkle with the sugar, salt and a trickle of the oil and roast in a preheated oven at 180°C (350°F) Gas 4 for 2 hours until nearly dried out.

Meanwhile, heat the rest of the oil in a frying pan/skillet, add the breadcrumbs and, when they start to brown, add the garlic and parsley. When they are lightly brown all over, strain off the excess oil through a sieve and sprinkle the crumbs over the tomatoes.

When ready to serve, reheat them in a preheated oven at 200°C (400°F) Gas 6 for 15–20 minutes.

roast summer vegetables

The joy of this dish is that you need not stick to the same selection of vegetables as here. Mushrooms, new potatoes and carrots all roast well in a medley. You can also ring the changes with different herbs and spices. An endlessly adaptable dish.

1 small aubergine/eggplant, or
3–4 Japanese aubergines/eggplants

4 small red onions

1 sweet potato

3 tablespoons olive oil

8 cherry tomatoes

2 bell peppers, red and/or yellow

2 medium courgettes/zucchinis or 1 small soft-skinned squash

1 whole head of garlic, separated into cloves, but unpeeled

1–2 large sprigs of rosemary or thyme

sea salt and freshly ground black pepper

serves 4

Slice the aubergine/eggplant into bite-sized wedges, quarter the onions, peel the sweet potato and cut it into chunks.

Put the aubergine/eggplant, onions and sweet potato in a plastic bag, add the oil and shake gently until everything is well coated. Transfer them all to a roasting tin and sprinkle with salt. Add the tomatoes and turn to coat with the oil.

Roast in a preheated oven at 230°C (450°F) Gas 8 for 15 minutes while you prepare the other vegetables.

Remove the stalks from the peppers and the seeds and ribs from the inside. Slice the flesh into thick wedges or chunks. Trim the courgettes/zucchinis and cut them lengthways into quarters and again in half if they are too long. Deseed the squash and cut it into chunks.

Add the peppers and courgettes/zucchinis to the roasting pan, turning them all in the oil. Tuck in the garlic and rosemary and return the pan to the oven for another 15 minutes. Lower the oven temperature to 180°C (350°F) Gas 4 and cover the tin with foil. Remove the foil after 15 minutes. If there is too much liquid in the tin, continue roasting uncovered for a final 10 minutes or so.

Serve as an antipasto, as an accompaniment to roast meats, or with chunky bread and other dishes as a light lunch.

roast pumpkin and garlic polenta

Polenta normally has lavish amounts of butter and cheese added to give it flavour, but here's a much lighter version made with roast pumpkin and roast garlic, which you can cook at the same time as your main roast.

1 medium pumpkin or 1 large butternut squash

5 large garlic cloves, unpeeled

3 tablespoons sunflower/safflower or grapeseed oil

40 g/2½ tablespoons butter

50 g/½ cup Parmesan cheese, grated, plus extra to taste

1.2 litres/2 pints vegetable stock, plus a little extra as necessary

250 g/1⅔ cups good-quality Italian polenta

sea salt and freshly ground black pepper

serves 6

Preheat the oven to 190°C (375°F) Gas 5. Halve the pumpkin. Cut one half into quarters and scoop out the seeds. Quarter the other half, scoop out the seeds, cut each quarter into 2 or 3 pieces and cut away the skin with a sharp knife. Put all the pumpkin in a roasting pan along with the garlic cloves. Drizzle with the oil, mix well together and season generously with salt and pepper. Roast in the preheated oven for about 35–40 minutes until soft.

Remove the quartered pumpkin from the pan and set the rest aside to be reheated just before serving. Scrape the flesh off the skin and place in a food processor. Pop the roasted garlic cloves out of their skins and add to the pumpkin and whizz until smooth. Add the butter and Parmesan, whizz again and season with salt and pepper.

Cook the polenta in the vegetable stock, following the instructions on the packet, taking care to whisk well to avoid lumps. Add the pumpkin and garlic purée to the cooked polenta and mix well. Add a little extra stock if needed to give a slightly sloppy consistency. Check the seasoning, adding more salt, pepper and Parmesan to taste. Reheat the pumpkin pieces briefly in a microwave or frying pan/skillet. Serve topped with pumpkin pieces.

roast butternut squash

Arguably the best-tasting squash and deep gold when roasted, butternut squash is an ideal accompaniment to so many dishes. If you roast it at a high heat, it will brown like a potato, or when cooked more gently, it marries well with fresh herbs.

1 large butternut squash or 2 small ones

2 tablespoons olive oil

75 g/6 tablespoons unsalted butter

a bunch of fresh thyme, tips snipped into sprigs

2 garlic cloves, sliced

sea salt and freshly ground black pepper

serves 4–8

Cut the squash in half lengthways and scoop out the seeds and pith with a spoon. Cut each half into 3–4 wedges, according to the size of the squash. There is no need to peel them.

Put the oil and butter in a roasting pan and heat on top of the stove until melted. Add the wedges of butternut and baste the pieces, turning them carefully to cover. Push the sprigs of thyme and slices of garlic between the wedges and sprinkle with salt and pepper.

Roast in a preheated oven at 190°C (375°F) Gas 5 for 30 minutes, turning the pieces over a couple of times to brown them lightly as they finish cooking.

Variation Peel the wedges of butternut with a potato peeler or turning knife. Bring a large saucepan of salted water to the boil, add the wedges, return to the boil and simmer for about 5 minutes. Drain well. This initial par-boiling seasons them with salt and and gives a crunchy exterior.

pumpkin roasted with sage and onion

Pumpkin is a favourite vegetable throughout Italy, and is generally made into soup or ravioli filling. However, if the flesh is not too watery, it is delicious roasted in olive oil on a bed of sage and sliced onions.

750 g/1½ lb. fresh butternut squash pumpkin

6 tablespoons extra virgin olive oil

2 large onions, sliced

12 fresh sage leaves

a pinch of chilli/hot red pepper flakes

1 tablespoon red wine vinegar or balsamic vinegar

sea salt and freshly ground black pepper

serves 4

Scoop the seeds out of the squash and cut away the skin. Cut into long slices or chunks.

Pour 4 tablespoons olive oil into a metal or enamel roasting pan and add the onion. Season with salt and pepper and toss well to coat. Scatter the pumpkin over the onion and the sage leaves over the pumpkin. Drizzle with the remaining olive oil and season with chilli/hot red pepper flakes, salt and pepper.

Roast in a preheated oven at 220°C (425°F) Gas 7 for 25–30 minutes until tender and beginning to brown. Remove from the oven, sprinkle with the vinegar while it is still hot, then serve.

baby squash stuffed with pine nuts, currants, lemon and herbs

The flavours here are Italian in style, specifically Sicilian, and I love the unexpected mix of sweet currants with the saltiness of the capers and cheese. The lemon and mint lifts the whole thing. This is lovely served either warm or at room temperature. A Greek-style salad with some tomatoes, feta cheese and red onion would work perfectly as an accompaniment.

4 small acorn squashes or 4 good-sized courgettes/zucchinis (about 18–20 cm/ 7–8 inches long)

1 tablespoon salted capers

30 g/1 oz. currants

1 medium onion, finely chopped

5–6 tablespoons extra virgin olive oil

2–3 garlic cloves, finely chopped

120 g/4½ oz. fresh white breadcrumbs

2 tablespoons chopped flat leaf parsley

2 tablespoons chopped mint leaves

1–2 teaspoons grated lemon zest

50 g/½ cup Parmesan cheese, freshly grated

50 g/½ cup pine nuts, lightly toasted

1 medium egg, beaten (optional)

1 tablespoon freshly squeezed lemon juice

sea salt and freshly ground black pepper

serves 4

If using acorn or other small summer squash, just cut off a thin slice from the base so that they stand upright without wobbling, then cut off a lid and scoop out the seeds to make a cavity. If using courgettes/zucchinis, halve them lengthways and, using a teaspoon, remove the seeds in the centre to leave a 'boat' shape. Season the cut surfaces with salt and leave them upside down to drain. In two separate bowls, cover the capers and currants with warm water and leave them to soak.

When the squashes or courgettes/zucchinis have drained for 45–60 minutes, rinse them, pat dry, then steam for 10–12 minutes until just tender. Drain well on paper towels. Preheat the oven to 190°C (375°F) Gas 5.

Meanwhile, gently fry the onion in 2 tablespoons of the oil with a pinch of salt until soft and sweet, about 10–15 minutes. Add the garlic and cook for another 3–4 minutes. Drain the capers and currants. Mix the onion and garlic with all the other ingredients except the egg, remaining oil and lemon juice. Season to taste. Stir in the egg for a firmer stuffing, if desired. Put the squash or courgettes/zucchinis in a baking dish and fill the cavities with the stuffing. Mix together the remaining oil and lemon juice and spoon it over the vegetables. Bake in the preheated oven for 30–35 minutes, basting once, until golden and crisp on top. Serve warm with a Greek-style salad.

cauliflower gratin

A regular accompaniment on the *plat du jour* circuit, this recipe goes especially well with pork. The secret of delicious cauliflower is to blanch it first; if you parboil it with a bay leaf, the unpleasant cabbage aroma disappears.

1 large cauliflower, separated into large florets

1 fresh bay leaf

500 ml/2 cups double/heavy cream

1 egg

2 teaspoons Dijon mustard

160 g /1½ cups finely grated Comté cheese*

coarse sea salt

a baking dish, about 25 cm/10 inches diameter, greased with butter

serves 4–6

Bring a large saucepan of water to the boil, add the bay leaf, salt generously, then add the cauliflower. Cook until still slightly firm, about 10 minutes. Drain and set aside.

Put the cream in a saucepan and bring to the boil. Boil for 10 minutes, then stir in the mustard and 1 teaspoon salt.

Divide the cauliflower into smaller florets, then stir into the cream sauce. Transfer to the prepared dish and sprinkle the cheese over the top in an even layer. Bake in a preheated oven at 200°C (400°F) Gas 6 until golden, about 40–45 minutes. Serve hot.

Note Like Gruyère, Comté is a mountain cheese – from the Franche-Comté region to be precise – but the similarity stops there. Comté's distinct flavour comes from the milk used in the making, so the flavour varies with the seasons. A springtime diet of tender young shoots delivers milk that is very different from its winter counterpart, nourished mainly on hay. I've never met a Comté I didn't like, but it is darker in colour and fruitier in summer, paler and more nutty in winter. Use Emmental or Cantal if it is unavailable.

cavolo nero

This versatile vegetable is a popular ingredient in many classic Italian dishes, from soups to salads, but is also makes a fantastic accompaniment to roast meat and fish dishes.

3 heads of cavolo nero or spring greens

3 tablespoons olive oil

1 garlic clove, thinly sliced

sea salt and freshly ground black pepper

serves 6

Pull the leaves off the stalks and tear out the central tough rib of each leaf.

Slice the greens and put in a saucepan. Pour over just enough boiling water to cover, bring back to the boil and cook for 2–3 minutes. Drain the greens.

Add the oil to the saucepan and cook the garlic very gently without colouring until soft and sweet (about

5 minutes). Toss the greens in the garlic-flavoured oil and cook over low heat for 5 minutes. Season to taste and serve as soon as possible.

slow-cooked Brussels sprouts with pancetta and chestnuts

Brussels sprouts (first cultivated many, many years ago in Flanders) are a member of the cabbage family. They look just like little baby cabbages and are especially sweet, tender and tasty when they are young. Use baby sprouts in this rather festive dish, which is just as lovely on its own or as a side with roast pork, baked ham or turkey. These are also delicious served with Roast Beef (page 24).

200 g/6½ oz. fresh chestnuts

60 ml/¼ cup light olive oil

50 g/2 oz. pancetta, chopped into 1-cm/½-inch pieces

1 small onion, finely chopped

2 garlic cloves, thinly sliced

60 ml/¼ cup chicken stock

60 ml/¼ cup dry white wine

1 tablespoon freshly squeezed lemon juice

400 g/14 oz. Brussels sprouts, trimmed

serves 2

Preheat the oven to 200°C (400°F) Gas 6.

Cut a small slit, without cutting into the flesh, along one side of the chestnuts. Put them on a baking sheet and roast in the preheated oven for 15–20 minutes, until the skins start to split. Remove from the oven and let cool a little. Peel and rub off the skin and set aside.

Heat the oil in a heavy-based saucepan over medium heat. Add the pancetta, onion and garlic and cook for 3–4 minutes. Pour in the stock, wine and lemon juice and bring to the boil. Add the sprouts to the pan, cover, reduce the heat and simmer gently for 20 minutes.

Carefully turn the sprouts over and add the chestnuts to the pan. Cover and cook for a further 20 minutes, until almost all the liquid has evaporated. Serve immediately.

French beans with garlic

French beans are the classic accompaniment for lamb, but they are equally nice with fish and chicken. You can also serve at room temperature, as part of a salad buffet. Instead of the cooked beans, try long, thin slices of steamed courgettes/zucchinis, sautéed with the garlic.

625 g/1½ lb. small green beans, trimmed

2 tablespoons extra virgin olive oil

1 tablespoon unsalted butter

2 garlic cloves, crushed

a handful of flat leaf parsley, chopped

1 teaspoon freshly squeezed lemon juice (optional)

coarse sea salt and freshly ground black pepper

serves 4

Bring a large saucepan of water to the boil. Add the beans and cook for 3–4 minutes from the time the water returns to the boil. Drain and refresh under cold running water. Set aside.

Heat the oil and butter in a frying pan/skillet. Add the garlic, beans and salt, and cook on high for 1 minute, stirring. Remove from the heat and stir in the parsley and lemon juice, if using. Sprinkle with pepper and serve.

Variation Flageolet beans are the other traditional partner for lamb. Generally, dried beans taste better if cooked from scratch, but this does require advance planning. Happily, I find that flageolets are the exception, especially if you can find imported French flageolets in jars, not cans. For mixed beans to serve with lamb (for four), halve the quantity of green beans and add a 400 g/14-oz. jar of drained beans to the cooked green beans when frying with the garlic. Instead of lemon juice, stir in 3–4 tablespoons crème fraîche or cream just before serving.

Danish red cabbage

It is all the extras traditionally served with a roast turkey that turn it into a feast, as well as making the bird 'go further' for what is often a very large family gathering. Danish Red Cabbage is a traditional accompaniment for roast goose, pork or duck, as its sweet and sour flavours complement the meat.

1 red cabbage, about 1.5 kg/3 lb.

50 g/4 tablespoons unsalted butter, plus extra to taste

1 tablespoon brown sugar

freshly squeezed juice of ½ lemon or 1 tablespoon vinegar, plus extra to taste

125 ml/½ cup cherry or blackcurrant juice

serves 4

Cut the cabbage into quarters. Remove the stem and shred the leaves finely.

Melt the butter in a large saucepan, then stir in the sugar over gentle heat. Add the lemon juice and half the cherry juice, then bring to the boil. Add the cabbage and turn to coat in the liquid. Reduce the heat to low, then cover and steam until tender, about 2 hours, stirring frequently and adding more cherry juice if necessary.

Remove the saucepan lid for the last 15 minutes, then taste and add a lump of butter and extra lemon juice if the cabbage is too sweet.

roast stuffed apples

Rich roasts, such as pork, goose or duck, are traditionally served with accompaniments that are both sweet and sour. They used to be popular wintertime celebration dishes, so seasonal or stored ingredients were used. Cabbage is a winter crop, and apples were stored in racks for winter use. The apples and prunes used to stuff the goose are sometimes too fatty to eat, so these prune-stuffed roast apples are an alternative.

4 small Bramley or other sour cooking apples

16 Agen prunes, cooked and pitted

¼ teaspoon ground cinnamon

4 teaspoons unsalted butter, melted

olive or sunflower/safflower oil, for brushing

serves 4

Core the apples, then make a shallow cut around the 'equators' so they don't explode in the oven. Brush oil over the skins with a pastry brush. Stuff each core with a cooked prune. Sprinkle with the cinnamon and push 1 teaspoon butter into each hole.

Bake in a preheated oven at 160–180°C (325–350°F) Gas 3–4 for 50 minutes–1 hour until the apples are tender but still keep their shape.

the trimmings

chestnut stuffing

If you have favourite sausages, such as Toulouse, use them in this stuffing, otherwise ordinary sausage meat is perfectly good. This mixture is much lighter without added breadcrumbs or egg, and is ideal for stuffing the neck of a turkey or goose.

400 g/14 oz. fresh chestnuts (200 g/ 7–8 oz. peeled and cooked) or 200 g vacuum-packed chestnuts, ready peeled and cooked

250 ml/1 cup milk (if using fresh chestnuts)

100 g/4 oz. sausages or sausage meat

2 tablespoons olive oil

1 onion, chopped

150 g/6 oz. turkey liver, chopped (if unavailable, use chicken livers)

60 g/2 oz. streaky/fatty bacon slices, finely chopped

1 tablespoon chopped fresh flat leaf parsley or marjoram (optional)

sea salt and freshly ground black pepper

makes about 500 g/I lb.

If the chestnuts are fresh, they must first be boiled to soften the shell, then peeled while still hot (protect your fingers with rubber gloves).

Put the peeled fresh chestnuts in a saucepan, cover them with the milk and simmer gently until softened, probably 30 minutes but it can take up to 1 hour if they are old ones. Strain them if necessary, weigh out 200 g/7 oz. and put in a bowl.

Crumble the cooked chestnuts with your fingers and use the sausage meat to bind them.

Heat the oil in a frying pan/skillet, add the onion, liver and bacon slices and fry gently until the liver is firm. Stir in the parsley and cook until the mixture begins to brown. Add to the chestnuts with salt and pepper to taste.

Note This and other stuffings used in this book may also be cooked separately from the bird. Form into balls and cook in a baking dish at 200°C (400°F) Gas 6 for about 20 minutes.

lemon and herb stuffing

This makes a succulent hot stuffing. It is also very good when cold and tastes even better the next day, when it will have become firm and easy to slice.

2 eggs

125 g/1 stick plus 1 tablespoon butter, melted

a handful of fresh parsley leaves

1 teaspoon lemon thyme

freshly grated zest and juice of 1 unwaxed lemon

225 g/4½ cups fresh white breadcrumbs

sea salt and freshly ground black pepper

makes enough for a large chicken or small turkey

Put the eggs, butter, parsley, thyme, lemon zest and juice in a blender and work to a smooth purée. Pour it over the crumbs and mix well. Season to taste with salt and pepper.

apricot stuffing

This fruity stuffing works well with turkey or goose.

60 g/¼ cup onions, chopped

60 g/¼ cup cashew nuts

2 celery stalks, coarsely chopped

75 g/⅓ cup dried apricots, soaked in 75 ml/ ¼ cup water

100 g/7 tablespoons unsalted butter

60 g/1¼ cups fresh white breadcrumbs

freshly grated zest of 1 unwaxed orange

freshly squeezed juice of ½ lemon

makes about 500 g/2½–3 cups

Put the onions, cashew nuts, celery and apricots in a food processor. Blend until evenly chopped.

Melt the butter in a saucepan and add the chopped onion mixture. Cook until the nuts begin to brown, then add the crumbs, zest and juice. Transfer to a bowl and let cool. Stuff the bird. If there is any left over, form into cakes and fry in butter in a small frying pan/skillet.

salami stuffing

This recipe uses pre-roasted, peeled, vacuum-packed chestnuts. If using fresh chestnuts prepare as in recipe on page 222.

60 g/3 oz. vacuum-packed chestnuts*

40 g/1 cup fresh breadcrumbs

100 ml/½ cup chicken stock

2 tablespoons olive oil

1 garlic clove, crushed

30 g/1½ oz. chicken livers

60 g/3 oz. Italian salami, chopped

60 g/3 oz. button mushrooms, chopped

1 teaspoon freshly squeezed lemon juice, diluted with 1 tablespoon water

2 teaspoons chopped fresh sage

1 egg yolk, beaten

freshly ground black pepper

makes enough for a large chicken or small turkey

Put the chestnuts in a bowl and crumble them with a fork or between your fingers. Add the crumbs and stir in the stock.

Put the oil and garlic in a small frying pan/skillet and heat until the garlic begins to brown. Add the livers and salami, fry for 30 seconds, then add the mushrooms and diluted lemon juice. Stir well and cook for another 2 minutes or until most of the water has evaporated. Season with plenty of pepper and add the sage, moist breadcrumbs and chestnuts. Remove from the heat, let cool for 5 minutes, then stir in the beaten egg yolk.

gravy

This is a thickened gravy for beef which should lightly coat the meat and vegetables.

1 tablespoon fat from the pan

1 onion, thinly sliced

250 ml/1 cup good beef stock

2 teaspoons cornflour/cornstarch, mixed with 2 teaspoons cold water

sea salt and freshly ground black pepper

serves 4–6

Put the roasting pan on top of the stove, heat the reserved 1 tablespoon fat, add the onion and cook slowly over low heat until browned, about 30 minutes. Do not let burn. Add the stock and cornflour/cornstarch mixture, then season to taste with salt and pepper. Stir constantly over low heat until the mixture boils and simmer for a couple of minutes. Strain if you wish or serve as it is.

wine gravy

A classic gravy for any kind of roast – use wine (or brandy) to deglaze the pan, scraping up all the delicious sediments.

2 tablespoons fat from the pan

4 tablespoons red wine

1 tablespoon plain/all-purpose flour (or more if you like a thicker gravy)

500 ml/2 cups well-flavoured stock or water

sea salt and freshly ground black pepper

serves 4–6

Put the roasting pan on top of the stove, heat the reserved 2 tablespoons fat, add the wine and reduce to 3 tablespoons. Add the flour, stir well until there are no more flecks of white, then pour in the stock or water. Stir constantly over low heat until the mixture boils. Season with salt and pepper. Strain into a clean saucepan if necessary, reheat and serve.

bread sauce

A classic sauce to serve with turkey.

½ onion, finely chopped

½ teaspoon dried thyme

3 whole cloves

500 ml/2 cups milk

100 g/3½ oz. fresh white breadcrumbs

75 g/¾ stick unsalted butter (optional)

2 tablespoons double/heavy cream (optional)

sea salt and freshly ground black pepper

serves 8–10

Put the onion, thyme, cloves and milk in a saucepan. Bring gently to the boil over low heat. Simmer for 5 minutes. Remove from the heat and set aside for 1 hour. Remove the cloves.

Add the breadcrumbs, butter and cream, if using, to the pan. Reheat until nearly boiling. Stir well, then add salt and pepper to taste. Set aside for 10 minutes to thicken, then reheat if necessary before serving.

horseradish sauce.

1 large horseradish root
1 tablespoon white wine vinegar
250 ml/1 cup double/heavy cream
sea salt

makes about 500–600 ml/2–2½ cups, serves 6–8

Scrape the fresh horseradish root clean and grate it finely to give 2 tablespoons.

Put in a bowl, add the vinegar and salt and stir well. Add the cream and whisk until it becomes thick and light. Rest it at room temperature for at least 2 hours, but serve the same day.

cranberry relish

100 g/2 cups fresh cranberries
100 ml/a scant ½ cup cider vinegar
about 3 cm/1 inch fresh ginger, grated
½ cinnamon stick
2 juniper berries, crushed
2 cloves
50 g/½ cup demerara sugar

makes about 250 ml/1 cup

Pick over the cranberries and put them in a saucepan. Add the vinegar, ginger, cinnamon, juniper berries and cloves and simmer until the berries begin to break, adding water if it looks like drying out.

Add the sugar and cook for about 20 minutes more. Remove the cloves and cinnamon stick. Check the consistency – it should be like a loose jam. If not, simmer a little longer.

cherry salsa

2 tablespoons sugar

200 ml/1 cup red wine

50 ml/3 tablespoons balsamic vinegar

500 g/1 lb. cherries, pitted

serves 4

Put the sugar, red wine and balsamic vinegar in a saucepan and heat until the sugar has dissolved.

Add the cherries and simmer gently for 1 hour or until the juice has reduced to at least a quarter of its original volume. Remove from the heat and let cool.

Using a slotted spoon, transfer the cherries to a small bowl and serve. Discard the juice.

salsa verde

1 tablespoon chopped fresh chives

1 tablespoon chopped fresh coriander/cilantro

1 tablespoon chopped fresh flat leaf parsley

1 tablespoon grated fresh ginger

at least 20 sorrel leaves, sliced

freshly squeezed juice of ½ lemon

2 tablespoons olive oil

½ teaspoon salt

serves 4

Mix all ingredients together in a bowl and warm in a microwave on HIGH/100 per cent for 10 seconds. Serve warm.

romesco sauce

2 red bell peppers

100 ml/½ cup olive oil

2 garlic cloves

1 fresh red chilli, deseeded and sliced

200 g/7 oz. canned plum tomatoes

25 ml/1½ tablespoons red wine vinegar

1 tablespoon ground hazelnuts

1 tablespoon ground almonds

1 teaspoon salt

serves 4

Char the peppers under the grill/broiler, put in a paper bag, seal and let steam for 10 minutes. Remove the skin, seeds and membranes. Heat 1 teaspoon of the oil in a non-stick pan, lightly brown the garlic, then add the chilli and tomatoes. Dry out the mixture over high heat so it starts to fry and brown a little. Transfer to a blender, add the vinegar and remaining oil, and purée until smooth. Stir in the nuts to thicken the sauce. Add salt to taste.

bacon rolls

These are a traditional part of a British Christmas dinner served with turkey.

rindless bacon slices, preferably smoked streaky/fatty (see serving quantities)

metal skewers

6 slices bacon serves 2 people

Cut the bacon slices in half crossways. Roll the bacon up tightly into rolls and spear them on metal skewers – 6 per skewer. Roast in a preheated oven at 200°C (400°F) Gas 6 for 5 minutes, at the same time as the chipolatas.

chipolatas

Chipolatas come in as many varieties as regular sausages, but look more appetizing to serve as garnishes. They are often used to add extra filling to make an expensive dish go further, so allow at least two per person, and occasionally four.

2–4 chipolatas (venison if possible), per person

1 tablespoon cooking fat from the turkey

2–4 per person

Put the sausages in a small roasting pan, add the oil and turn to coat. Roast while the turkey is resting in a preheated oven at 200°C (400°F) Gas 6 until brown on one side. Turn them over and cook the other side. The total cooking time should be about 10 minutes.

sausage meat patties

Simplicity itself to make and a tasty accompaniment to roast chicken or turkey. Add a pinch of dried mixed herbs or Spanish smoked paprika, if liked.

85–150 g/3 oz–5½ oz. fresh sausagemeat per person

plain/all-purpose flour, for dusting

olive oil, for frying

2–3 patties per person

Take portions of the sausage meat about 1½ tablespoons each and roll into balls. Flatten them between your palms, then put on a clean work surface and dust with flour on both sides.

Heat the olive oil in a large frying pan/skillet, add the patties, spaced well apart, and in batches if necessary. Fry until brown and crisp on one side, then turn them over and brown the other side, about 5 minutes in total.

Yorkshire pudding

The traditional British Yorkshire pudding used to be served at the beginning of the meal to fill people up and make the meat 'go further'. These days, it acts as a mop for the gravy and pan juices. If you're lucky enough to have leftovers, they are delicious served for breakfast the next day with crisp-fried bacon and maple syrup.

275 ml/1 cup plus 1 tablespoon milk

2 whole eggs

125 g/¾ cup plain/all-purpose flour

½ teaspoon salt

4–6 tablespoons fat from the roasting pan

serves 6

Put the milk, eggs, flour and salt in a bowl and whisk well.

Heat the fat on top of the stove in one large pan or divide between 6-holes/cups (1 tablespoon fat each) or 12-holes/cups (½ teaspoon fat). Pour in the batter (take care because it will spatter).

Cook in a preheated oven at 230°C (450°F) Gas 8 until well risen (35 minutes for the large tin or 15 minutes for the individual pans). Serve as soon as possible.

index

recipe credits

Sonia Stevenson
Text on pages 8–21
Roast beef with all the trimmings
Fillet of beef and mushrooms wrapped in Palma ham
Roast boned beef loin basted with wine gravy
Roast stuffed topside with mustard and green peppercorns
French-carved rib steak
Slow-roasted breast of veal
Veal with mustard cream
Slow-roasted pork loin with rosemary, Madeira and orange
Spiced roast ham or pork with juniper berries
Rolled pork roast with sage and onion stuffing
Roast pork fillets with creamy Thai-spiced sauce
Loin of pork with a herb crust
Italian roast leg of lamb with lemon and anchovy sauce
Rack of lamb with cranberry sauce
Slow-roasted lamb shanks with chillies
Sonoran spiced orange chicken
Quick-roasted chicken pieces with tomatoes, mushrooms and brandy on crusty croutes
Spatchcocked poussins with rosemary and lemon glaze
Roast turkey with lemon and herb stuffing
Rolled turkey breast with spinach, bacon and cheese
Roast duck à l'Alsacienne with sauerkraut and frankfurters
Roast duck with cherry salsa
Scandinavian roast goose
Boned, rolled and stuffed pheasant breasts with whisky
Roast rabbit with herbs and cider
Marinated roast venison
Tuna with paprika crumbs and romesco sauce
Roast salmon fillets with sorrel sauce
Marinated sea bass with paprika and spices
Oven-roasted red snapper with sorrel and salsa verde
Roast cod cutlets on a base of thyme and lemon
Roast potatoes

Hasselback potatoes
Sweet potatoes en brochette
Glazed roast carrots
Fennel roasted in butter
Roast apples and celeriac or parsnips
Roast red onions
Roast whole heads of garlic
Roast mushrooms with olive oil and pine nuts
Crunchy roast garlic tomatoes
Roast summer vegetables
Roast butternut squash
Danish red cabbage
Roast stuffed apples
Chestnut stuffing
Lemon and herb stuffing
Apricot stuffing
Salami stuffing
Gravy
Wine gravy
Bread sauce
Horseradish sauce
Cranberry relish
Bacon rolls
Chipolatas
Sausage meat patties
Yorkshire puddings

Valerie Aikman-Smith
Indian spiced leg of lamb cooked in a salt crust with raita
Jasmine-brined roasted poussins with salsa verde
Crispy roast duck with Asian greens

Ghillie Basan
Honey-roasted spiced lamb
Roast chicken stuffed with couscous, apricots and dates
Baked trout stuffed with dates

Fiona Beckett
Roast fillet of beef with soy and butter sauce
Pot roast brisket with Zinfandel
Tuscan-style roast veal with wild mushrooms
Roast pumpkin and garlic polenta
Cavolo nero

Maxine Clark
Pork loin roasted with rosemary and garlic
Roast loin of pork with balsamic vinegar
Pot roast leg of lamb with rosemary and onion gravy

Chicken with forty cloves of garlic
Pheasant roasted with vin santo, grapes and walnuts
Tuna steaks baked with rosemary
Seabass baked in parchment
Braised whole globe artichokes
Pumpkin roasted with sage and onion

Ross Dobson
Roast beef ribeye with café de Paris butter and aparagus
Slow-cooked spiced pork belly with apple and fennel
Roasted pork with apple and fennel puddings
Shoulder of lamb with roasted vegetables
Brined roast chicken with a ham and fresh sage stuffing
Roasted spring chicken with herbs and ricotta
Roast turkey breast with olive salsa verde
Roast ducklings wth orange and ginger pilaf
Stuffed giant mushrooms with feta and herbs
Slow-cooked Brussels sprouts with pancetta and chestnuts

Clare Ferguson
Shoulder of lamb with mountain herbs

Brian Glover
Baby squash stuffed with pine nuts, currants, lemon and herbs

Alastair Hendy
Pot-roasted game bird with apple, cabbage, juniper and cream

Fran Warde
Crunchy roast pork with baked stuffed apples
Butterflied leg of lamb with Mediterranean stuffing
Roast chicken with lemon, thyme and potato stuffing
Roast duck with citrus fruits
Roasted pheasant breasts with bacon, shallots and mushrooms

Laura Washburn
Braised pot roast with red wine, rosemary and bay leaves
Meatloaf
Marinated pork roast
Guinea fowl with lentils
Roasted provençal salmon and vegetables with rouille
Whole roast monkfish
Creamy potato gratin
Carrots with cream and herbs
Cauliflower gratin
French beans with garlic

Lindy Wildsmith
Italian roast guinea fowl with new potatoes and green beans

photography credits